An interpretation of Keats's

Endymion

H. Clement Notcutt

Alpha Editions

This edition published in 2019

ISBN : 9789353861193

Design and Setting By
Alpha Editions
email - alphaedis@gmail.com

An Interpretation
of Keats's
Endymion

By

H. CLEMENT NOTCUTT

PROFESSOR OF ENGLISH
IN THE UNIVERSITY
OF STELLENBOSCH
SOUTH AFRICA

A careful study of *Endymion* made some ten years ago led to the conclusion that there was more of allegorical significance in the poem than had hitherto been recognised, but the effort to trace that significance was only partially successful. Further study since that time has gradually opened up the way to the interpretation that is worked out in the following pages. It is probable that there are details in the story the meaning of which still lies hidden, but it may at least be hoped that enough has been discovered to win for the poem its rightful place among the not very numerous examples in English poetry of well-wrought allegory.

It will be seen that frequent reference has been made to Sir Sidney Colvin's recently-published *Life of Keats* (second edition, 1918), which has superseded all other authorities on the subject; and, while the interpretation of *Endymion* here put forward differs largely from his treatment of that poem, it is pleasant to have the opportunity of giving expression to the deep sense of gratitude which all lovers of Keats must feel for his scholarly and sympathetic work.

STELLENBOSCH, SOUTH AFRICA,
10*th March*, 1919.

" It is a strange habit of wise
humanity to speak in enigmas
only, so that the highest truths
and usefullest laws must be
hunted for through whole
picture-galleries of dreams,
which to the vulgar seem
dreams only."

Ruskin.

An Interpretation
of Keats's
Endymion

I T is generally agreed that in writing *Endymion* Endymion an allegory.
Keats intended to do something more than
merely to re-tell an old legend.   He does
not appear, so far as the records go, to have
left any definite statement to that effect, but
there are indications that point distinctly to such a
purpose.   The poem beginning " I stood tiptoe upon
a little hill," with which his first volume, published
in March, 1817, opens, had originally been called
Endymion,[1] but was afterwards left without a title
because Keats had decided to make a more ambitious
effort to handle the same subject; and the significant
fact for our present purpose is that the earlier *Endymion*,
while it touches lightly upon the old legend, is really
concerned with the views of Keats on the philosophy of
poetry.   It would not then be surprising to find that the
longer and more ambitious treatment of the story, upon
which he set to work as soon as the earlier volume had
appeared, embodied his views on the same subject,
handled this time in a fuller and more elaborate manner.
It is perhaps worth noting how much of his verse is
concerned with this one theme—the training and function
of the poet.   In the volume of 1817, besides " I stood
tiptoe," the epistles to his brother George, to Mathew,

1 Letter to Charles Cowden Clarke, Dec., 1816.

and to Cowden Clarke, and the more important *Sleep and Poetry*, all deal with this matter; and in one of his latest pieces of work, *The Fall of Hyperion*, he returns once more to the same theme. It is interesting also to find his thoughts on other matters running into the form of allegory during the time when he was working on the first book of *Endymion*. In May, 1817, he writes to Taylor and Hessey (who afterwards published the poem) that he " could make a nice little allegorical poem called ' The Dun,' where we would have the Castle of Careless-ness, the Drawbridge of Credit, Sir Novelty Fashion's ex-pedition against the City of Tailors, etc., etc.," and turns immediately afterwards to the subject of *Endymion*. Lastly it may be noted that there is a passage in the first book which might of itself almost settle the question of the real significance of the poem. It occurs in the talk of Endymion with Peona (769 sq.), and in it the mask is for the moment laid aside, and Keats himself speaks out in his own proper person. He asks " Wherein lies happiness?" and goes on to answer :

> In that which becks
> Our ready minds to fellowship divine,
> A fellowship with essence, till we shine
> Full alchemiz'd, and free of space.   (I. 777)

He proceeds to mark off the various grades of happiness, starting from the sympathy that can enter into the wonders and aspirations of former days, and passing on through friendship to love, which may " produce more than our searching witnesseth " (834). And if earthly love, he goes on to say, can lift us far above the ordinary level of life, what power must lie in a passionate endeavour to reach up to a divine ideal ! It is fortunate that a record remains showing that Keats attached particular importance to this passage. The lines quoted

2

above were not in the original poem,[1] and in sending them to his publisher, as the poem was passing through the press, he wrote :

"You must indulge me by putting this in, for setting aside the badness of the other, such a preface is necessary to the subject. The whole thing must, I think, have appeared to you, who are a consecutive man, as a thing almost of mere words, but I assure you that, when I wrote it, it was a regular stepping of the Imagination towards a truth. My having written that argument will perhaps be of the greatest service to me of anything I ever did. It set before me the gradations of happiness, even like a kind of pleasure thermometer, and is my first step towards the chief attempt in the drama."[2]

It is evident, then, that there was much more in the mind of Keats when he wrote this poem than the re-telling of an old and fantastic tale. But, of course, the final justification for this view of *Endymion* must lie in the poem itself. If, as it is hoped to show, there is to be found, running beneath the surface of the poem in a clear and unbroken stream, a meaning that corresponds closely with the ideas that are known to have filled the mind of Keats at this time, there will be no need of further argument on the matter. An allegory of this kind does not slip into a poem by accident.

But, it may fairly be asked, why did not Keats Why Keats did not explain it. himself do something to elucidate the meaning of a poem which, though it cost him so much effort, seems to have been understood by few, if indeed by any, in his own

---

1 The original reading was as follows:
    Wherein lies happiness? In that which becks
    Our ready minds to blending pleasurable:
    And that delight is the most treasurable
    That makes the richest Alchymy. Behold, etc.

2 Letter to John Taylor, 30th January, 1818.

time, and which, even at this late day has scarcely yielded up its full treasure of meaning?

Two facts may supply a sufficient answer to this query. The first is that before he had finished the poem Keats became dissatisfied with and tired of it. This feeling shows itself repeatedly in his letters. Soon after he had reached the end of the third book he wrote to Haydon :

" My ideas with respect to it I assure you are very low—and I would write the subject thoroughly again—but I am tired of it and think the time would be better spent in writing a new Romance which I have in my eye for next summer."[1] And some time later to Reynolds : " I have copied my Fourth Book, and shall write the Preface soon. I wish it was all done; for I want to forget it, and make my mind free for something new."[2] And then the unintelligent and unfair criticism with which the poem was received by most of those who noticed it, and, what was almost worse, the indifference of the greater part of the literary world, would offer but a slender inducement to enter upon an explanation of its meaning. If even the few friends who took up his defence failed to interpret it rightly, what could be expected from those who began to read it with minds prejudiced against the author? So he held his peace. He probably felt as unwilling to explain his allegory as a humorist would be to explain one of his jokes that had fallen flat, and moreover he would know that any such defence would only give occasion for fresh ridicule.

The main intention.

Accepting the presence of an allegory as a working hypothesis we may next try to define its main intention. It is true that any attempt to state in matter-of-fact prose

1 Letter of 28th September, 1817.
2 Letter of 14th March, 1818: see also letter to John Taylor, 27th February, 1818, and to James Hessey, 9th October, 1818.

4

the significance of an allegory must inevitably be unsatisfactory. A painting of a sunset or of waves breaking on the shore is unsatisfactory, for how can one reproduce on canvas the constantly shifting play of light and colour which makes the real beauty of the scene? Yet we find pleasure in the attempt, and in the case of the allegory, where a more purely intellectual element is involved, an attempt to define its purpose has a real value in clearing one's way towards an understanding of the problems involved.

Professor de Sélincourt[1] has described the allegory Definitions as representing "the development of the poet's soul towards a complete realisation of itself." Mr. A. C. Bradley says[2]: " The adventures of Endymion are also the experiences of the poetic soul in its search for union with the absolute Beauty." Sir Sidney Colvin gives a fuller definition[3]: " The essence of Keats's task is to set forth the craving of the poet for full communion with the essential spirit of Beauty in the world, and the discipline by which he is led, through the exercise of the active human sympathies and the toilsome acquisition of knowledge, to the prosperous and beatific achievement of his quest."[4]

Each of these writers however proceeds to remark and criticisms upon the imperfect way in which the intention has been carried out. Professor de Sélincourt, after a brief

1 *Poems of John Keats*, Introduction P. xl.
2 *Chamber's Cyclopedia of English Literature*, vol. III., p. 100.
3 *Life of Keats*, p. 235. There is a briefer definition on p. 167
4 In his essay on the poems of Keats (1914), Mr. Robert Bridges says: " In so far as the poem has an inner meaning, Endymion must be identified with the poet as Man. The Moon represents ' Poetry ' or the Ideality of desired objects, *The Principle of Beauty in all things*: it is the supersensuous quality which makes all desired objects ideal; and Cynthia, as moon goddess, crowns and personifies this, representing the ideal beauty or love of woman: and in so far as she is also actually the Moon as well as the Indian lady—who clearly represents real or sensuous passion—it follows that the love of woman is in its essence the same with all love of beauty." But the section dealing with *Endymion* is not the happiest part of Mr. Bridges' essay.

sketch of the purpose of the poem, adds : " It is hardly safe to give a more detailed interpretation of the allegory, for, as a whole, *Endymion* is vague and obscure."[1]   Sir Sidney Colvin, while in some places taking up a more thorough going attitude of defence than previous writers had adopted, yet says : " In *Endymion* Keats had impeded and confused his narrative by working into it much incident and imagery symbolic of the cogitations and aspirations, the upliftings and misgivings, of his own unripe spirit :"[2] and quotes with approval Shelley's remark : " I think if he had printed about fifty pages of fragments from it, I should have been led to admire Keats as a poet more than I ought, of which there is now no danger."[3] Mr. A. C. Bradley is more severe : " The result is a series of adventures to the details of which it is impossible to assign a distinct symbolic meaning, and which, taken more simply, have the incoherence of a broken dream."[4]

That there are many faults of expression, and not a few lapses from good taste in all the earlier work of Keats, cannot be denied, and *Endymion* is by no means free from these defects; but it is hoped to show that there is a fuller and more consecutive meaning running through the whole poem than has yet been recognised; that many of the details which have been thought to be superfluous and unmeaning are significant and appropriate when viewed from the right standpoint; and that much of the criticism that has been directed against it is mistaken and irrelevant, since it is based upon a failure to understand the meaning and purpose of the passages criticised.

1 As above.
2 *Life of Keats*, p. 410.
3 Ibid, p. 238.
4 As above.

In trying to arrive at a satisfactory statement of the underlying meaning of the poem it is necessary to recognise that the allegory appears to have a double purpose— to carry at once a wider and a narrower meaning; the wider meaning having reference to the new birth of poetry which came about as soon as the power of the pseudo-classical school declined, and English poetry was released from what Keats regarded as the cramping and deadening influence that Pope and his associates had exercised; the narrower being intended to give some account of the experience of an individual, picturing the rise and development of the poetic passion in his mind, his earnest pursuit and gradual realisation of the ideal that is set before him. In some parts of the poem the two ideas can be recognised side by side, but usually one or the other is dominant for the time. Thus in the first book the earlier part is a picture of the spirit of the time in which the revival of poetry began, while the rest of the book deals with the more personal aspect of the subject.

One need not be surprised to find this double purpose at work. Keats was an enthusiastic admirer of Spenser, and the *Faerie Queene* would furnish him with a precedent that would be warrant enough for such a plan. It would indeed have been difficult to keep the two ideas apart from one another, for the impulses that were stirring in the mind of Keats, and were urging him on to develop his own gift of song, were but part of the great tidal movement that was flooding in through many channels; and he was clear sighted enough to recognise the fact. If we look at the sonnet that he addressed to Haydon in a letter of November, 1816;

Great spirits now on earth are sojourning,

in which he refers to Wordsworth, Leigh Hunt and Haydon himself as pioneers of a new era, and then read another letter addressed to Haydon in the following May, when working at *Endymion*, in which he quotes the opening lines of *Love's Labour Lost*:

> Let Fame, that all pant after in their lives,
> Live register'd upon our brazen tombs
> And so grace us in the disgrace of death;

and adds: " To think that I have no right to couple myself with you in this speech would be death to me," we can see how he thought of his own ambitions and ideals as connected with the wider movement that he saw to be in progress, not as a matter of boasting, but as the recognition of simple fact.

It may further be noted that the same collocation of ideas is to be found in *Sleep and Poetry*, which had been published a little while before he seriously took up the writing of *Endymion*.   In this poem he had denounced, in terms that roused the wrath of Byron, those who went about

> Holding a poor decrepid standard out
> Mark'd with most flimsy mottos, and in large
> The name of one Boileau!

and had gone on to celebrate the advent of happier times —" Now 'tis a fairer season :" and then had linked with all this the hope that he himself might be found worthy to play some part in this great poetic revival.

We may now try to ascertain what light can be gained on the purpose of the poem from a closer examination of the text.

BOOK I.

The story, so far as it is developed in the first book, falls into two clearly marked divisions; the first of these, covering about one-third of the total length of the book (lines 63 to 393) describes the festival of Pan; the second (lines 393 to 992) deals with the strange experiences which have changed the life of Endymion. It will be convenient to consider these separately.

It is on the side of Mount Latmos, near the western coast of Asia Minor, that the festival is about to be held. On the slopes of the mountain lay a dense forest, into some parts of which no man had penetrated (67). Sometimes a lamb, straying away from the flock to which it belonged, would be lost in the depths of the forest, but it was believed that such a lamb would be shielded from harm until it joined the herds of Pan, and that the shepherd who had lost it would gain thereby (78). There were many paths in the forest leading to a wide lawn, in the midst of which stood an altar (90). To this spot, early in the morning of a summer day, a troop of children came, and gathered round the altar, and as they stood expectant a faint breath of music came to their ears (114). Soon there appeared a troop of maidens and of shepherds, then a venerable priest, followed by more shepherds, and a joyous multitude accompanying a chariot drawn by three steeds, in which rode Endymion their prince. They were gathered round the shrine, while the priest exhorted them to join in giving thanks to Pan for all the benefits they had received. After sacrifice and libation a hymn to Pan was sung (232), and then many of those present joined in dancing and sports, while others allowed their minds to dwell on thoughts and images called up by what was going on around them, and as they played or meditated the sun arose in all his glory (350). On one side sat a group of old men, who were talking with one another about the next life, the duties that lay before them and the hopes of reunion with those they had loved.

The meaning. It may be admitted at the outset that this earlier part of the first book is not the most hopeful part of the poem in which to attempt the tracing of the allegory. As an introduction to the story it is simple and effective, but indications that would point out the purpose beneath the surface of the narrative are not easy to find. By making use, however, of clues to be found in later parts of the poem we can arrive at a fair degree of certainty as to the intention of this earlier part.

A widespread poetic feeling. It appears, then, that we have here shown to us in the manner of a picture the feeling that was abroad among men at the time when the new romantic movement began to exercise its influence. It is not only in the mind of the poet that such a movement stirs and grows; there must be a stirring, too, in the minds of many others who will never be poets, and they must be ready to share in the new ideas and emotions in such degree as they are capable of. For some time past men had paid little heed to the beauty of the world around them. As Wordsworth had put it when Keats was twelve years old:

> Little we see in Nature that is ours;
> We have given our hearts away—a sordid boon!
> This Sea that bares her bosom to the moon;
> The winds that will be howling at all hours,
> And are up-gathered now like sleeping flowers—
> For this, for everything, we are out of tune;
> It moves us not.

And it was a true charge that the old priest made when he said

> " Our vows are wanting to our great god Pan." (I. 213)

But a change was coming over the minds of men. They were tired of the wrangling and the strife, the insincere compliment and the bitter jibe that made up so large a

10

part of what poets had for a long time been saying to them; they were eager to respond to Wordsworth's invitation—

> Come forth into the light of things,
> Let Nature be your teacher.

They were ready to join in the desire that this new spirit of delight in and wonder at all that is beautiful and mysterious in Nature might spread among mankind : they could sing :

> be still the leaven
> That spreading in this dull and clodded earth
> Gives it a touch ethereal—a new birth :
> Be still a symbol of immensity ;
> A firmament reflected in a sea ;   (I. 296)

The main purpose of this opening part of the story is to show the new movement as one that was shared by many people; young and old, men, women and children were alike stirred by it, and the suggestion at the back of the story is that the change that came about in the world of poetry at this time was not merely the result of new ideas and a fresh outlook on the part of the poets; it was the expression of a spiritual change that had taken place in the minds of large numbers of people.   The revelation had come to the poet, as we shall see, in a way that was intimate and personal, and no one else could directly share in it, but there were many who, though quite unable to receive such a revelation as had come to him, still felt the throbbing of new impulses, and shared in the new joy.

The revival of the worship of Pan stands for the fresh interest in and love of nature which were widely diffused at the time of the poetic revival; and bearing this in mind a further significance may be recognised in some of the details of the story.   It will be remembered that a marble altar (90) stood in the middle of the wide lawn The altar and the lawn. (82) where this festival took place, and that there were many paths leading through the forest to this spot.   It

would appear that Keats intended to remind us th
reverence for Nature is no new thing; this part of t
great domain of poetry had been opened up long befoi
many paths led to it and had been trodden by worshippe
in earlier times; the altar that they had built, though
had been neglected for some time, still stood there rea
for the worshippers when they were willing to gath
round it. It may be noted, too, that it was before sunr
that the multitude came together to renew their vows
Pan, and then

> from the horizon's vaulted side,
> There shot a golden splendour far and wide,
> Spangling those million poutings of the brine
> With quivering ore: 'twas even an awful shine
> From the exaltation of Apollo's bow;
> A heavenly beacon in their dreary woe.   (I. 349)

So the beginning of the freshly-awakened interest
Nature, as it may be seen in the poems of Thomson a
Collins and Gray, showed itself before the sunshi
splendour of the new movement as it shone forth in t
time of Wordsworth and Coleridge.

It is difficult, if not impossible, to mark w
accuracy the limits of significance intended by the p(
in the details of his allegory. One cannot, for instan
be certain whether or not he meant the mighty for(
outspread upon the sides of Latmos to represent t
realm of poetry as a whole, and the

> gloomy shades, sequestered deep,
> Where no man went   (I. 67)

to stand for some portions of that realm which Ke
thought of as still remaining to be occupied; themes
aspects of life which were awaiting the poet of the futu
in contrast with the lawn into which many paths led a
where stood the altar to Pan, at which many poets h
sacrificed. But there are a few lines, not in the m
current of the story, in which we shall probably not

far wrong in recognising a partly personal reminiscence, also aside from the direct line of the allegory. They refer to the lamb that sometimes strayed far down those inmost glens (69) and never returned to join the flocks;

> but pass'd unworried
> By angry wolf, or pard with prying head,
> Until it came to some unfooted plains
> Where fed the herds of Pan : ay great his gains
> Who thus one lamb did lose. (I. 75)

It seems likely that Keats was thinking of the fate of some of his own poems. There were many lambs in the white flock of his first published volume that had been worried by the angry wolves or pards with prying head who howled in the pages of the *Eclectic Review*[1] and other periodicals at Leigh Hunt and all who were suspected of being his friends. But there were other poems that he did not publish, some perhaps had not even been put into writing,[2] and these were never (in his lifetime, at any rate) gathered into the pens that held the main flock. Keats, regarding them in a way with which Browning would have fully sympathised,[3] felt that these poems had not perished, but had joined the herds of Pan, and that the gain to him was great for they lived on in his mind as beautiful ideals, unmarred by foolish or unfriendly criticism. There is, of course, no need to suppose that Keats intended to limit the application of the parable to his own experience. Many a poet must have had a similar feeling about his unpublished poems.

1 See Colvin, *Life of Keats*, p. 132.
2 Cf. the sonnet " When I have fears that I may cease to be," written in January, 1818, before *Endymion* was published.
3 Cf. *Abt Vogler*:
" There shall never be one lost good! What was, shall live as before.
All we have willed or hoped or dreamed of good shall exist;
Not its semblance but itself; no beauty, nor good, nor power
Whose voice has gone forth, but each survives for the melodist
When eternity affirms the conception of an hour."

Thus far we have followed the story of the festival of Pan. It remains to consider the latter part of the first book which tells of the experiences through which Endymion had passed and which had caused such a marked change in his demeanour. In earlier days he had been foremost in all active exercises, but now he seemed to be oppressed by some secret grief, and could not join in the festivities of the day (393). His sister Peona drew him from the crowd and took him to a quiet retreat, where, under her restful influence, he fell asleep (442). When he awoke refreshed and grateful for her sisterly affection, he told her the cause of the change that had come upon him. He had seen a vision of surpassing loveliness (572), and though it was but a dream, and had passed away, leaving him desolate, it had been followed by a second appearance of the same bright face, mirrored in a clear well (895). This was no dream, for he saw it with waking eyes, but it too, had quickly vanished. Finally, as he was one day following the course of a stream, he had reached a quiet and beautiful cave (935), and, as he longed with a great longing for the presence of the unknown goddess whom he had come to love so deeply, he heard her voice calling him, and realised that she was with him once more. But those moments had quickly fled, and, feeling now the hopelessness of his passion, he declared that he would put his grief aside, and return to a quiet and wholesome life.

In this part of the story it is not difficult to trace Keats's own reminiscences of the way in which there gradually grew up within him the conviction that he must devote himself to the pursuit of poetry, until that became at length the one absorbing passion of his life.

Endymion's days, as he himself tells us, had until recently been marked by healthy activity; he was full of

14

energy, and delighted in manly exercises; he was one—

> Who, for very sport of heart, would race
> With [his] own steed from Araby; pluck down
> A vulture from his towery perching; frown
> A lion into growling. (I. 533)

And Keats, according to the account of his school friends, showed a similar disposition in his early days. One of them, Mr. Edward Holmes, has left the following record : " Keats was in childhood not attached to books. His *penchant* was for fighting. He would fight anyone— morning, noon and night—his brother among the rest. It was meat and drink to him . . . . . He was not literary : his love of work and poetry manifested itself chiefly about the year before he left school. In all active exercises he excelled."[1]

But a change had come over Endymion; he no longer took any interest in the manly sports that had hitherto been his chief delight; he had lost all his " toil breeding fire " (537) and at times he became oblivious of all that was going on around him :

> he did not heed
> The sudden silence, or the whispers low,
> Or the old eyes dissolving at his woe,
> Or anxious calls, or close of trembling palms,
> Or maiden's sigh, that grief itself embalms :
> But in the self-same fixed trance he kept,
> Like one who on the earth had never stept. (I. 398)

So Keats pictures to us the change that comes over a man's outlook on life when once he has heard the call to devote himself to the pursuit of poetry. Hitherto he has led a life not differing in any marked way from the life of his fellows; he has joined in the same pursuits, and has shared in their interests and pleasures. But when once he has caught a glimpse of an ideal loftier and more beautiful than anything that has hitherto entered into his conception of life, he cannot go on as before. The old

His love of poetry awakened

---

1 Colvin, *Life of Keats*, pp. 11, 12.

pursuits and pleasures seem empty and meaningless; h
becomes absorbed in the contemplation of the new ideal
it fascinates him, and alters his whole attitude to life
Endymion speaks of " the change wrought suddenly i
me " (I. 520), and, though it is not for a long time tha
he fully makes up his mind to devote himself to the pur
suit of the new ideal, it is clear that Keats intends us t
think of the experience that resulted in the new outloo
upon life as having taken place on some definite an
identifiable occasion. It may further be noted that th
experience is a rare one. Not many men are called t

be poets, and in the story it is Endymion alone of al
the people who sees the vision and hears the call. Fo
the most part the people around him are quite unabl
to enter into his feelings, though there are a few of mor
sympathetic understanding, who are able to share a littl
in them;

> he seem'd
> To common lookers on, like one who dream'd
> Of idleness in groves Elysian:
> But there were some who feelingly could scan
> A lurking trouble in his nether lip
> And see that oftentimes the reins would slip
> Through his forgotten hands: then would they sigh,
> And think of yellow leaves, of owlets' cry,
> Of logs piled solemnly.   (I. 175)

This isolation of the poet, the solitariness of the path tha
he has to follow through life, is a point frequently insiste
upon in the allegory. It is a pathetic illustration of th
limited degree of sympathetic understanding with whic
the poet must expect to meet that when Keats read 1
Wordsworth this beautiful hymn to Pan—a crystal vas
containing as a distilled essence the very flower (
Wordsworth's own teaching—all the comment that h
passed upon it seems to have been that it was " a pret
piece of paganism "—Wordsworth, who had himse
declared that he would " rather be a pagan suckled :

16

a creed outworn " if only his eyes and ears might be open to the beauty and mystery of the world around him. If this was all the appreciation that Wordsworth had to offer it seems unreasonable to speak severely of the obtuseness of later critics, and even the Quarterly Reviewer should be pitied rather than blamed.

The story of the three-fold revelation that was The three-fold revelation. granted to Endymion is skilfully worked out. It is obviously intended to represent the growth in a man's mind of the consciousness that he is called to be a poet. It may be true that the poet is born not made, but at any rate he is not conscious of the fact when he is born, nor for some time after. He may arrive at the consciousness in various ways, but Keats represents it here as coming to him first of all on a few definite occasions, and in such a way that, from the time when the idea first dawned upon him, his whole outlook upon life was changed, even though some considerable time went by before he finally made up his mind to devote his life to this one purpose.

There are four aspects of this part of the story that appear to be specially significant, and these may now be considered.

1. In the first place it will be noticed that some The first vision in a familiar spot stress is laid on the fact that when the new revelation came to Endymion he was in a place that he had often been accustomed to visit. On the first occasion he was on the border of a wood, where the river winds round it, and there he had made his way to a nook, *where he had been used to pass his weary eves* (546), and from which he had often watched the beauty of sunset; and it was here, heralded by the sudden blossoming of a magic bed of flowers that the vision came to him.

In the account of the second revelation this feature and the second of the story is dwelt upon at greater length. It was

in a deep hollow, overarched by bushes and trees, wher
some mouldered steps led down to the margin of a wel
(870).   From there he had often brought flowers t
Peona; there, too, he would " bubble up the wate
through a reed," or make ships

> Of moulted feathers, touchwood, alder chips,
> With leaves stuck in them; and the Neptune be
> Of their petty ocean.   (I. 882)

When in a less childish mood he often sat there

> contemplating the figures wild
> Of o'er-head clouds melting the mirror through.   (I. 886).

It may be regarded as one of the canons in th
interpretation of allegory that if apparently dispropor
tionate stress is laid upon any aspect of the story ther
is probably enshrined in it something of special signifi
cance in the allegory.   In a carelessly constructe
allegory this will not, of course, hold good, but the mor
one examines this poem the more evidence one finds tha
the thinking has been close and consecutive, and tha
while the expression is in places immature and faulty
the conception is fine, and much more carefully worke
out than has yet been admitted.

In this instance, the meaning is not difficult to trace
and it is of sufficient importance to justify the stress lai
upon the matter.   Keats appears to be telling us some
thing of what led up to his realisation of the wonderfu
beauty of real poetry.   As a child he had, no doub
often heard or read and probably learned, poems or part
of poems; he had, perhaps, amused his sister in her bab
days by repeating these to her, just as in later days h
wrote nonsense rhymes for her;[1] he may very likely hav
imitated verses of the great poets, picking up a feathe
moulted from one of their poems, a chip from the
workshop, and making out of it a little craft of his ow

---

[1] See, for example, letter of 2nd July, 1818.

18

In later days he would sit pondering on the way in which life is mirrored in such works.   And it was here, on ground long familiar to him, in poems that he had known from childhood, that there came to him suddenly and unexpectedly a vision of the indescribable beauty that inspires all really great poetry.   It is not an uncommon experience.   Many of us have learned in childhood poems that have given us some degree of pleasure at the time, and then in later years we have one day found in them a charm of form and meaning that we had never realised before.   There is granted to us a glimpse of the beauty of poetry in itself, and we share in some small degree in the experience of Keats; but it is only a very few who are capable of seeing it as he saw it, or in whom it can arouse such an intensity of wonder and delight that it inspires them to make an *Endymion* of it.

In contrast with the familiarity of the ground on The third on new ground which Endymion had met with these experiences, we find that the spot where the third revelation came to him is not spoken of as one of his earlier haunts.   This time he had been—

> hurling [his] lance
> From place to place, and following at chance,   (I. 929),

till at last it struck through some young trees and fell into a brook, which led him to a cave; and the description suggests that all this part of the forest was new to him. It may well have been the case that after Keats had twice been surprised by the recognition of some unearthly beauty in poems that had for a long time been familiar to him, he began to read more widely, to wander at random through the realms of gold, and that in some place that he hit upon almost by chance there came to him again, and more clearly than before, the sense of the surpassing loveliness to be met with in poetry.

2. A more obvious point than the one dealt with above is the solitary character of these experiences. On each occasion Endymion was wandering quite alone when the revelation came to him, and this suggests one aspect of the experience through which the poet must pass. The inspirations that come to him, the visions of beauty that he sees, are intensely personal and individual experiences. Even if his days should be spent in a crowded city, in his poetic life no one can go with him; he may tell the story of it to others, but they can never share it; the vision is for him alone.

3. A point that is well worked out is the progressive character of these experiences. Endymion's attention was first of all caught by a sudden blossoming of flowers in a familiar spot. He pondered over it until his head was dizzy and distraught (565). At length he fell asleep and then there came the vision, first of the moon:

> She did soar
> So passionately bright, my dazzled soul
> Commingling with her argent spheres did roll
> Through clear and cloudy: (I. 593)

and when she vanished there came in her place one who seemed the " high perfection of all sweetness " (607). " Yet it was but a dream." (574).

On the second occasion he was sitting near the well when a cloudy Cupid flew by, and he was just about to follow it when he saw—

> The same bright face [he] tasted in [his] sleep
> Smiling in the clear well. (I. 895)

There is no suggestion this time of the distraction and confusion of mind that marked the former occasion, and moreover, the vision appears to him, not when he is asleep, but in his waking hours, and is followed by indications of the divine favour that are unmistakable.

The third appearance comes when he is consciously longing for the presence of her who has become his ideal,

20

and it shows a further advance in the fact that on this occasion he hears a voice calling to him, and is granted a fuller and more intimate revelation than before. Thus Keats has represented to us the way in which the poet gradually comes to a fuller realisation of what it is that he is called to do. He sees more and more clearly the beauty of the ideal that is set before him, and is filled more and more with a longing to attain it. It will be seen that a further stage in the realisation of the ideal is represented in the next book (II., 714-827), while the final consummation is reached at the end of the poem.

4. Between these times of exaltation Endymion sank into a mood of deep depression that gradually subsided into a quiet state of resignation as he made up his mind to put aside all thoughts of the ideal that seemed so impossible of attainment, and tried to resume his ordinary life; and then this contentment would be broken up by a fresh vision. This alternation between joyous hope and black despair is, of course, characteristic of the artistic temperament, and is one of the penalties that the poet has to pay for the sensitiveness without which he could not be a poet; but one cannot help suspecting that personal reminiscence has played a large part in this phase of the story.

And this brings us to the consideration of a question Is Keats describing his own experience? that cannot but arise as one endeavours to follow out the meaning of this poem—the question, that is, as to how far the experiences of Endymion represent the training and development of the poet in general, and how far they correspond to the personal experiences of Keats.

The question is one that can never be fully answered. Keats himself is the only one who could have told us how far he was drawing upon memories of what he himself had gone through, and he has not spoken. Of his letters that have come down to us, only twenty-four belong to the period before he had finished *Endymion*, and these throw no direct, and but little indirect light on the problem.

On the other hand a little consideration serves to show that in dealing with such a theme he must inevitably have drawn mainly upon his own experience. The only poet whose mind he could know with sufficient intimacy was himself. He was indeed friendly in varying degrees with Leigh Hunt, with Shelley and with Wordsworth, and it is quite possible that in the many talks that Keats enjoyed with one or another of these—talks of which a few faint echoes have reached our ears—some ideas may have been thrown up that have been built into the structure of *Endymion*. Be this as it may, one can hardly doubt that the story of Endymion's effort to win the prize that was set before him is drawn in the main from the recollections that filled the mind of Keats of his own hopes and doubts and difficulties, and there are some parts of the story in which the identification is clear.

The resemblance between the Endymion of the days before the visions, when his delight was in the exercise of physical energy, and Keats in his earlier schooldays when he excelled in all active exercises, and was not literary, has already been pointed out;[1] and the parallel is the more striking because there is no reason whatever to suppose that it was in the mind of Mr. Holmes when he wrote down his recollections of Keats as he knew him at the age of fourteen. No less striking is the evidence

[1] See above, page 15.

22

of the change that came over Keats in the course of the next five or six years.   Henry Stephens, one of the medical students who shared a room with him in London, has described his point of view in those days : "Poetry was to his mind the zenith of all his aspirations : the only thing worthy the attention of superior minds : so he thought : all other pursuits were mean and tame.   He had no idea of fame or greatness but as it was connected with the pursuits of poetry or the attainment of poetical excellence."[1]   If the free and active life of Endymion in his earlier days is a reflection of the way in which Keats felt when he was fourteen, it is equally clear that the visions of divine beauty that came to Endymion after-wards, and the rapture that they aroused in him, represent the feelings with regard to poetry and poetic fame that at this later period dominated the mind of Keats.   Of the intervening period there is scarcely any record, but one can feel little doubt that when we read the story of the way in which Endymion passed from the heights of enthusiasm to the depths of depression, and of the efforts that he made to recover a normal and reasonable frame of mind,[2] we are learning of the inner experiences of the poet.   Between the time of his leaving school (about August, 1811) and the day when he dropped his medical studies and finally made up his mind to devote himself to poetry (about March, 1817), he must have passed through many periods of doubt and uncertainty, of longing to reach the ideal that he saw shining before him, of despair at the poor prospects of attaining to it when he realised the feebleness of his own early efforts. He must have decided more than once to put it all on one side and to fall in with the wishes of those of his

1 Colvin, *Life of Keats*, p. 31.
2 See, for example, Book I., 691-710, and 913-927.

friends who were urging him to complete his medical studies : " No more," says Endymion to Peona,

> will I count over, link by link,
> My chain of grief : no longer strive to find
> A half-forgetfulness in mountain wind
> Blustering about my ears : aye, thou shalt see,
> Dearest of sisters, what my life shall be ;
> What a calm round of hours shall make my days.
> There is a paly flame of hope that plays
> Where'er I look : but yet, I'll say 'tis naught—
> And here I bid it die.   Have not I caught,
> Already, a more healthy countenance?"   (I. 978).

It is only in the pages of *Endymion* that the record of these perplexities and struggles may be found, but a late echo of them survives in a letter to Leigh Hunt, written in May, 1817, soon after he had begun to work at this poem :

"I vow that I have been down in the mouth lately at this work.   These last two days, however, I have felt more confident—I have asked myself so often why I should be a poet more than other men, seeing how great a thing it is—how great things are to be gained by it, what a thing to be in the mouth of Fame—that at last the idea has grown so monstrously beyond my seeming power of attainment, that the other day I nearly consented with myself to drop into a Phaeton."

A wider meaning.

It would, however, be a mistake to push this identification too far.   At certain points in the story, both in this book and later, it seems clear that Keats is drawing largely upon the memory of his own experiences in order to make his sketch more vivid and true; but it would misrepresent the purpose of the poem to suppose that Endymion regularly stands for Keats himself.   He embodies a more general conception, and his story is intended to picture for us the kind of experience through which any poet who is worthy of the name must pass; while at times he represents a still wider idea—that of the spirit of the new romanticism.

It remains to consider briefly the character of Peona, Peona. and her significance in the story. She is represented as being devotedly attached to Endymion. When the trouble of his mind so weighed upon him that he lost all consciousness of those about him, it was she who led him away and soothed him into a refreshing sleep. She watched over him while he slept, and when he awoke she sang to soothe him, and then begged him to tell her what it was that had so strangely altered his character. But when he had told her of his wonderful dream she quite failed to understand how such an experience could affect him so deeply :

> " Is this the cause?
> This all? Yet it is strange, and sad, alas!
> That one who through this middle earth should pass
> Most like a sojourning demi-god, and have
> His name upon the harp-string, should achieve
> No higher bard than simple maidenhood,
> Singing alone and fearfully. . . . (I. 721)

> how light
> Must dreams themselves be; seeing they're more slight
> Than the mere nothing that engenders them!
> Then wherefore sully the entrusted gem
> Of high and noble life with thoughts so sick?
> Why pierce high-fronted honour to the quick
> For nothing but a dream?" (I. 754)

Endymion replied with some energy, but even after he had told her of the two later revelations, Peona gave no sign that she was able to enter into his feelings, and her influence so far prevailed that he was ready, at any rate for the moment, to return to the normal life of healthy activity from which he had so strangely been drawn away.

Peona stands for a type of person whom we all know and admire. Simple, practical, unimaginative, but at the same time unselfish and affectionate, they form a most wholesome element in the scheme of life; we owe them more than we can tell. They have no glimpse of the

25

meaning or power of lofty and far away ideals; they believe in doing the practical duty that lies close at hand; they rejoice when they can draw the unpractical idealist down to the wholesome level of quiet everyday life, but when they fail to do this they are no less ready to hover round with ministering cheerfulness. They may at times express a gentle surprise at, or even disapproval of the wild unreasonableness of the dreamer, but the best of them, in whose number Peona may be reckoned, do not worry him, but, accepting the matter as being beyond their ken, retire into silent sympathy and practical helpfulness.

One cannot tell whether Keats had any actual person in mind in drawing the portrait of Peona. There is an interesting passage in a letter that he wrote to his friend, Bailey, not long after *Endymion* had appeared,

Georgiana
Keats.

in which he speaks of his brother George's wife. They had recently been married, and were on the point of leaving for America.

" I had known my sister-in-law some time before she was my sister, and was very fond of her. I like her better and better. She is the most disinterested woman I ever knew—that is to say, she goes beyond degree in it. To see an entirely disinterested girl quite happy is the most pleasant and extraordinary thing in the world. . . . Women must want imagination, and they may thank God for it."[1]

One may perhaps infer that Georgiana Keats had sat as an unconscious model for some of the features of Peona. But there is a passage in another letter, written to these young married people after they had settled in America, that puts the matter in a different light.

[1] Letter of 10th June, 1818.

" Your content in each other is a delight to me which I cannot express—the Moon is now shining full and brilliant—she is the same to me in Matter what you are to me in Spirit. If you were here, my dear Sister, I could not pronounce the words which I can write to you from a distance : I have a tenderness for you, and an admiration which I feel to be as great and more chaste than I can have for any woman in the world. You will mention Fanny [his sister]—her character is not formed, her identity does not press upon me as yours does."[1]

This suggests that some of the qualities that appear in the sketch of Diana were derived from the warm affection and admiration that Keats felt for Georgiana. His sister was at this time only fourteen years of age, and while the tone of warm affection in which Endymion speaks to Peona corresponds well with that pervading the really delightful letters that Keats both at this time and afterwards, wrote to her, we can hardly suppose that her opinion as to the wisdom or otherwise of his devoting himself to the life of a poet was very pronounced. It is not of course to be supposed that either Georgiana or Fanny is at all closely represented in the character of Peona, but it may well be the case ,as the passages quoted from his letters suggest, that the affectionate regard that Keats entertained for them was at the back of his mind in some parts of the story and influenced what he wrote.

It is, perhaps, worth noting that Mr. Locker- Fanny Keats. Lampson, who met Fanny many years later in Rome (she was married to Señor Valentine Llanos, a Spanish man of letters), found her, both in the matter of her affection for her brother John, and her failure to understand him, singularly like the Peona of the poem :

1 Letter to George and Georgiana Keats, October, 1818. Mrs. F. M. Owen in her study of Keats (Kegan Paul, 1880), drew attention to this letter, and its bearing upon *Endymion*.

" Whilst I was in Rome, Mr. Severn introduced me to M. and Mme. Valentine de Llanos, a kindly couple. He was a Spaniard, lean, silent, dusky and literary, the author of *Don Esteban* and *Sandoval*. She was fat, blonde, and lymphatic, and both were elderly. *She was John Keats's sister!* I had a good deal of talk with her, or rather *at* her, for she was not very responsive. I was disappointed, for I remember that my sprightliness made her yawn; she seemed inert and had nothing to tell me of her wizard brother of whom she spoke as a mystery —with a vague admiration but a genuine affection. She was simple and natural—I believe she is a very worthy woman."[1]

BOOK II.

The story.

In the second book we are taken down into a region away from all the stir and movement of human life. Endymion, wandering in the forest, is still in a restless and dissatisfied mood notwithstanding his promise to Peona, when his fancy is caught by a bud from which emerges a golden butterfly (61). He follows it, and is led to the mouth of a cavern, where a nymph, rising from a fountain, warns him that he has yet far to go before he can attain to what he is striving after (123). In response to a voice calling to him from the cavern he makes his way down, and finds himself in a strange, though beautiful region, from which all sign of human life has passed away. In the course of his wanderings he comes upon a temple with many ramifications (257); he is led into a chamber where he sees Adonis sleeping, and while he is there Venus comes and carries Adonis away (581); he

[1] F. Locker Lampson, *My Confidences*, p. 343: Quoted in Colvin's *Life of Keats*, p. 537.

28

passes some magic fountains and is delighted with the changing shapes that they assume (606); he has a vision of Cybele (640); and then, the path failing him, he is carried by an eagle to a quiet bower (670) where his long pursuit is rewarded by a fuller revelation of his heavenly love than has yet been granted to him.   After she has left him he sees the pursuit of Arethusa by Alpheus (936) and sympathises with their pains.   And suddenly he finds himself moving in the depths of the ocean.

Our study of the first book has led us to the conclusion that in the story of the strange experiences through which Endymion passed there is pictured the gradual awakening of Keats to the possibility that he might hope to achieve fame as a poet; and the black despondency that settled down upon him in the long periods of waiting between the somewhat rare occasions when his hopes shone brightly.   In the second book the story is continued.   The hope once awakened in him · could not be crushed by fears or hesitations, even though these might prevail for a time; and there is now set before us in picturesque form the process of training that had to be undergone in order that the poet might be made fit for the realisation of his ideal.

Sir Sidney Colvin has admirably described the way in which the mind of Keats naturally worked.   " When he conceives or wishes to express general ideas, his only way of doing so is by calling up, from the multitudes of concrete images with which his memory and imagination are haunted, such as strike him as fitted by their colour and significance, their quality of association and suggestion, to stand for and symbolize the abstractions working in his mind, and in this concrete and figurative fashion he will be found, by those who take the pains to follow him, to think coherently and purposefully enough."[1]

Its meaning. The images with which we meet in the second book may at first seem strange and bizarre; the winding passages of the underground world, the silver grots, the orbed diamond, the forsaken temple, the magic fountains —these may well be called wild and fantastic imaginations beneath which Keats has so effectively hidden his symbolic purpose, that readers, by no means unsympathetic, have been driven to doubt whether it is there at all. Even Sir Sidney Colvin, referring primarily to the description of the magic fountains that kept on changing their form, gives up the riddle and says : " This and much else on the underground journey seems to be the outcome of pure fancy and day-dreaming on the poet's part, without symbolic purpose."[2]

Yet one cannot but feel that it is unlikely that Keats would allow himself to wander aimlessly from the point in a poem dealing with a subject that was to him of all things most vital and sacred, especially when one bears in mind the fact that it was just through such images that his ideas seemed most naturally to find expression. One need not abandon the hope that even in the strange and fantastic symbolism of this book Keats " will be found, by those who take the pains to follow him, to think coherently and purposefully enough."

The meaning then that is suggested as underlying the symbolism of this book is mainly a personal one— Keats is continuing the story of his preparation for the work of a poet. He tells us how he could not put aside the longing that he might some day be found worthy of this high calling, however far away such an ideal might

1 Colvin, *Life of Keats*, p. 128.
2 Ibid, p. 186.

seem; and how, by what seemed a happy chance, he was led to enter upon an earnest and thorough study of some of the great classical poets. He tells us how fascinating he found the study, and yet how at times he was oppressed by·what seemed its deadness and want of relation to life as he knew it: and then we see how he came to recognise a greater beauty and significance in some of the old legends than he had hitherto perceived; and finally, he pictures the renewed assurance that came to him that he would one day reach the goal towards which he was striving.

We must now examine the details of the story with a view to ascertaining how far the interpretation here suggested is supported by them. Endymion has found himself unable to return to his former life of healthy activity as he had told Peona he would do; he cannot shake off the influence of the vision that has called to him again and again with growing clearness; and the interpretation of this part of the story follows naturally upon that which we have already recognised in the first book. When the idea of achieving fame as a poet had once laid hold of the mind of Keats he could not shake it off: he might at times, when the ideal seemed too far out of reach, resolve to turn back to medicine and surgery, and make a renewed effort to fit himself in the normal way for this profession; but the call of poetry became more and more insistent, and no effort of will, and no pressure from his guardian could drive it out of his mind.

The incident that breaks in upon his mood of The episode of the butterfly. depression leads on to the journey underground with which this book is mainly concerned. Endymion—

is sitting by a shady spring,
And elbow-deep with feverous fingering
Stems the upbursting cold : a wild rose tree
Pavilions him in bloom, and he doth see
A bud which snares his fancy : lo! but now
He plucks it, dips its stalk in the water : how!
It swells, it buds, it flowers beneath his sight;
And, in the middle, there is softly pight
A golden butterfly; upon whose wings
There must be surely character'd strange things,
For with wide eye he wonders, and smiles oft.   (II. 53)

Endymion follows this little herald as it flutters away, and in the pursuit his mood of languor is changed into eagerness. It leads him to the side of a fountain pouring out near the mouth of a cavern. As it sips from the stream it vanishes, but soon afterwards Endymion hears a voice calling to him, and looking round he sees the nymph of the fountain, who tells him that it is she who, in the form of the butterfly, has led him to this place,[1] and warns him that he has yet far to travel before he can hope to attain the object of his desires. She vanishes, and Endymion is left with a sense of perplexity and disappointment. He watches the moon, now shining brightly, and though he does not recognise her oneness with his divine visitant, his spirit is stirred with an intense longing; he feels that he is almost " sailing with her through the dizzy sky " (187), and, as his passionate desire grows almost too great to bear, he hears a voice calling to him from the cavern and bidding him descend.

Its meaning. The view that is to be taken of the meaning of this episode must depend on the interpretation that is given to the story of the underground wanderings of Endymion, to which it serves as an introduction. This will be considered in its place, but for the moment it may be

[1] This point has not always been understood, but it appears to be
a necessary inference from the text:
                all I dare to say,
    Is that I pity thee; that on this day
    I've been thy guide.   (II. 121).

taken as a working assumption that these wanderings are intended to represent the course of study in classical poetry that Keats carried on for some time.   With this as a clue one is led to recognise that Keats is here depicting an experience of which no other record remains, though we know that he must at some time have passed through it.   He was not much more than eight years old when he began to attend Mr. Clarke's school at Enfield, and how soon he took up the study of Latin we do not know; but we do know that at some period, probably during the last two years of his school life, classical story and poetry began to exercise a fascination upon him that is not usual in the case of a school boy; and we may gather that he is picturing to us his recollection of the occasion when he first felt this fascination.

The actual experience, vivid though it may have been in the recollection of Keats, is presented to us in a manner that makes it by no means easy to recognise the meaning of the details.   It reminds one of a photograph taken from an aeroplane, which, though concerned with actual and even familiar objects, shows them in a way that is difficult to interpret.   But, read in the light of the idea stated above, it appears to mean that on some occasion when Keats was deep in meditation, turning over the pages of some book, possibly Lemprière's Classical Dictionary, which as Cowden Clarke tells us he appeared to *learn* during the later months of his school life, he lighted upon some legend or story that " snared his fancy."   He read it and became interested in it, and, turning from the bare outline given in Lemprière (the bud) to the pages of Ovid or Virgil in which it was told at length with all the beauty of their verse, he found more charm and meaning in it than he had at first recognised (" it flowers beneath his sight "). He followed it up through the different writers that had touched it, and found the pursuit full of interest and pleasure.

"It seemed he flew the way so easy was." (II. 69)

At length the pursuit came to an end; the immediate interest of the story was exhausted, and he began to realise what it had to tell him with regard to his poetical ambitions. The story transformed itself into a warning. Delightful as he had found it, the little investigation that he had carried out had opened his eyes to the limitations of his own knowledge and he began to realise that he "must wander far in other regions" before he could hope to attain to his ideal. He felt discouraged. He had thought more than once that he was on the verge of the fulfilment of his hopes : he had encamped—

"To take a fancied city of delight" (II. 143)

only to meet with disappointment and failure. The verses that he had written could not, even in his own judgment, be called poetry. Yet he could not abandon hope; and as he dwelt upon the beauty of poetry in itself, the achievement of the poet loomed more and more glorious in his imagination until there seemed to be nothing else worth living for; and, realising that to become worthy of such achievement he must bury himself in a course of earnest and prolonged study, he resolved to enter upon it forthwith. "Oh, for ten years," cried Keats in another place—

"that I may overwhelm
Myself in poetry; so I may do the deed
That my own soul has to itself decreed."[1]

The journey underground. The rest of this book is concerned with Endymion's adventures underground, and it may be noted at the outset, as bearing upon the interpretation that has been

[1] *Sleep and Poetry*, 1. 96.

suggested, that the region through which he passes is one from which all human life has departed; there are some remains of man's handiwork, of which the shrine with the image of Diana is the most striking; but the impression left is that these courts and passages have long been silent and forsaken. They are a fitting symbol of the literature of an age long gone by. There are near the opening of this part of the story a few lines which it would be hard to match as a description of classical literature as a whole:

> Dark, nor light,
> The region: nor bright, nor sombre wholly,
> But mingled up; a gleaming melancholy,
> A dusky empire and its diadems;
> One faint eternal eventide of gems.   (II. 221)

The imperfect and partial understanding of these old writers, which is all that is possible in these latter days, together with the unfading, clear cut beauty of numberless passages in them, is suggested here with a skill and sureness of touch that Keats did not often attain to at this period of his work. When Tennyson tried to describe the kind of beauty that he had found in the classical poets he used the same image:

> " Jewels five words long
> That on the stretch'd forefinger of all Time
> Sparkle for ever."[1]

The pleasure that Endymion found in exploring this new region—

> "'Twas far too strange, and wonderful for sadness;
> Sharpening by degrees his appetite
> To dive into the deepest "—   (II. 219)

may be taken as a reminiscence of the delight with which Keats plunged into his classical studies when he had once begun to feel the fascination of them. " He was at work," says Cowden Clarke, " before the first school-hour

---

1 *The Princess*, Canto II., 355.

began, and that was at seven o'clock; almost all the intervening times of recreation were so devoted; and during the afternoon holidays, when all were at play, he would be in the school—almost the only one—at his Latin or French translation."[1]

The track that Endymion followed is described in some detail. We hear of " a vein of gold " (II. 226); " metal woof, like Vulcan's rainbow " (230); of—

> " silver grots or giant range
> Of sapphire columns, or fantastic bridge
> Athwart a flood of crystal." (II. 237)

The path leads along a track " with all its lines abrupt and angular " (228), now entering " a vast antre," where the " monstrous roof curves hugely " (231), now leading " through winding passages " (235) or crossing a ridge—"

> " that o'er the vast beneath
> Towers like an ocean cliff " (II. 240);

and the description suggests on the one hand the qualities that are characteristic of ancient classical poetry as con= trasted with that of the modern romantic school—the severity, the colder, harder kind of beauty; and on the other the great variety of interest and outlook to be met with as one passes from one to another of the great writers of Greece and Rome. A little later Endymion came in sight of—

The orbed diamond.

> an orbed diamond, set to fray
> Old darkness from his throne: 'twas like the sun
> Uprisen o'er chaos: (II. 245)

and the amazement that he felt in looking at it, so great that his bosom grew chilly and numb (243), reminds us of the feelings attributed to Cortez and his men, who

> " Look'd at each other with a wild surmise—
> Silent, upon a peak in Darien,"

1 Colvin, *Life of Keats.* p. 13.

36

and probably refers to the same experience, when Keats first looked into Chapman's Homer; and this interpretation is confirmed by the suggestion that the words carry of a light set to shine in a region that was all dark before. It is at this point, indeed, that Keats gives us a plain intimation of the meaning of the story, for he tells us that the wonders of this region are—

> past the wit
> Of any spirit to tell, but one of those
> Who, when this planet's sphering time doth close,
> Will be its high remembrancers: who they?
> The mighty ones who have made eternal day
> For Greece and England.   (II. 249)

Endymion now came to a temple   The temple.

> so complete and true
> In sacred custom that he well nigh fear'd
> To search it inwards.   (II. 257)

With feelings of awe he approached and looked " down sidelong aisles and into niches old " (264) and then

> began to thread
> All courts and passages, *where silence dead*
> *Rous'd by his whispering footsteps murmured faint*:
> And long he travers'd to and fro, to acquaint
> Himself with every mystery and awe.   (II. 266)

It seems likely that in the description of the minute and careful way in which Endymion examined this temple[1] Keats has embodied his recollections of his own study of Virgil's *Aeneid*.   Cowden Clarke tells us that he was so fascinated with this epic that before leaving school he had voluntarily translated in writing a considerable portion of it.[2]   Nor did his apprenticeship to

---

[1] Colvin (*Life of Keats*, p. 184) takes the latter part of this description to refer to some other building than the temple in which stands the image of Diana; but it seems better to regard the whole passage, down to line 270, as relating to the same temple. The fair shrine beyond which stands the quivered Diana is in the chief [hall] of the temple (I. 298).   Endymion first sees this " through a long pillar'd vista " (260), so that the temple is not a small building, and the other aisles and courts and passages may be naturally taken as forming part of it.

[2] Colvin, *Life of Keats*, p. 14.

37

Mr. Hammond lessen his enthusiasm, for " at Edmonton he plunged back into his school occupations of reading and translating whenever he could spare the time. He finished at this time his prose version of the *Aeneid*."[1] And the recollection must have been a pleasant one to have inspired such lines as those italicised above. One would have to seek far to find such a perfect description of the sensations aroused as one makes one's way with wonder and admiration through this great poem of days long gone by.

At length Endymion grew wearied and sat down " before the maw of a wide outlet " to think about what he had seen.

> There, when new wonders ceas'd to float before
> And thoughts of self came on, how crude and sore
> The journey homeward to habitual self! (II. 274)

If one tries to enter into the feelings of Keats when he had completed his translation of the *Aeneid* one can well imagine that he had become conscious of a new standard of poetical expression; he had begun to realise as he had never done before what a value belonged to the choice of the *mot juste* : he had felt—

> " All the charm of all the Muses
> often flowering in a lonely word; "

and he realised painfully how far his own attempts fell short of this standard; his verses would, indeed, seem " crude," his recognition of his own limitations might well make him feel " sore." His aspirations for poetic fame appeared—

> A mad pursuing of the fog-born elf,
> Whose flitting lantern, through rude nettle-briar,
> Cheats us into a swamp, into a fire. (II. 277)

But soon another feeling became more prominent. He was oppressed by the loneliness of the place and the

---

1 Colvin, *Life of Keats*, p. 18.

38

deadness of his surroundings. He longed to see the sky, the rivers, the flowers and the grass; he was cut off from all these things; he was in a region from which all life had departed, and the work to which he felt himself called could not be accomplished in such a place.

> " No!" exclaimed he, " Why should I tarry here?"
> " No!" loudly echoed times innumerable;   (II. 295)

for the romantic poets, great as was their admiration for the true classics, felt that they had to speak out a living message to a living world, and that no mere imitation of the methods of a by-gone age could accomplish this. So he returned into the temple, and reaching the shrine of Diana prayed to her that as she does not " waste her loveliness in dismal elements " (312) so he may be delivered from the rapacious deep and brought where he can " once more hear the linnet's note " (322). And in this passionate cry we may recognise a feeling in the mind of Keats that greatly as these works that he had been studying were to be admired for their perfection of form, their brilliance of expression, and their variety of interest, yet they belonged to another age, another race of men, and were lacking in fresh and living significance for the world of his day. But, as in answer to the prayer of Endymion, there sprang up through the marble floor of the temple a growth of leaves and flowers :

> Nor in one spot alone, the floral pride
> In a long whispering birth enchanted grew
> Before his footsteps—   (II. 345)

so Keats came to realise that the eternal principles of life might even yet find expression through the seemingly dead pages of these poets of a by-gone age.

Cheered by this assurance, which would remind him of the occasion when the first revelation of divine beauty was vouchsafed to him (I. 554 sq.), Endymion started off once more " increasing still in heart and pleasant sense "

(II. 351).   Before long he caught the sound of music, and he was deeply stirred.   It was a hopeful sign, and showed that his ear must now be more finely attuned to the melodies of heaven, for when this same supernatural music had before broken " in smoothest echoes through copse-clad vallies " (I. 119) it was only the children, the heralds of the coming day, who were given power to hear it.   So entranced was he by the music that it was only through the leading of " a heavenly guide benignant " that he passed safely through a thousand mazes till

Venus and
Adonis.

At last, with sudden step, he came upon
A chamber, myrtle wall'd, embower'd high,   (II. 388)

where lay Adonis, sleeping, guarded by Cupids.   Endymion, though " a wanderer from upper day " is welcomed, and is feasted with wine and fruit and manna, while there is told to him the story of the passion of Venus for Adonis, of the fate that befel him, and of the decree by which his death, " medicined to a lengthened drowsiness " was changed " each summer time to life."   Soon Venus herself comes down, and, after speaking words of encouragement to Endymion, carries Adonis away with her.   So ends this episode. It represents the fulfilment of the promise of the life that was to be discovered in these old legends. Keats is still trying by means of images " to symbolise the abstractions working in his mind," but the meaning of the images here is not obscure. He is telling us how, after he had first recognised that there was something more in these old legends than the dead perfection of an obsolete poetry, one of them at least blossomed out richly and filled him with delight. And while the revelation lasted, while the sense of the living truth embodied in the story was full upon him, the world of classic poetry no longer seemed dim and lonely; it was full of warmth and light and music and meaning. As Sir Sidney Colvin has remarked : " To

40

rescue the mind of England from this mode of deadness was part of the work of the poetical revival of 1800 and onwards, and Keats was the poet who has contributed most to the task. . . . It was his gift to make live by imagination, whether in few words or in many, every ancient fable that came up in his mind." He could " follow out a classic myth . . . . from a mere hint to its recesses, and find the human beauty and tenderness that lurk there."[1]

At length the inspiration passed :

> The earth clos'd—gave a solitary moan—
> And left him once again in twilight lone. (II. 586)

Endymion was greatly cheered by what he had seen :

> he felt assur'd
> Of happy times, when all he had endur'd   ,
> Would seem a feather to the mighty prize.
> So with unusual gladness on he hies. (II. 590)

And in these words we may take it that Keats is recalling the feeling of encouragement and pleasure with which, after the revelation that he has pictured for us above, he turned again to the study of the classics with a fuller assurance that he would gain from them guidance and inspiration for his poetical work.

The path that he follows is described by images similar to those in which the earlier part of the underground journey is set before us. He passes—

> Through caves and palaces of mottled ore,
> Gold dome, and crystal wall and turquois floor,
> Black polish'd porticos of awful shade,
> And, at the last, a diamond balustrade : (II. 594)

and the suggestion, as before, is that of a great and wonderful beauty, but a beauty that is hard and cold and without life, such as is usually felt to be the characteristic of the greater part of classical poetry.

1 Colvin, *Life of Keats*, p. 220.

But now Endymion comes upon a new marvel.
The path which he is following brings him—

The magic
fountains.

> just above the silvery heads
> Of a thousand fountains, so that he could dash
> The waters with his spear; but at the splash,
> Done heedlessly, those spouting columns rose
> Sudden a poplar's height, and 'gan to enclose
> His diamond path with fretwork streaming round
> Alive.   (II. 603)

Endymion dwelt long on the strangeness of the
scene, and the detail with which it is described suggests
that he gave to it the same close attention as he had
previously devoted to the temple which he had reached in
the earlier part of his wanderings. The whole description may at first appear fantastic in the extreme, but,
following the clue that has led us to this point, we
recognise that Keats is telling us how, after his study of
Virgil, he went on to make himself thoroughly acquainted
with the poems of Ovid, more especially with the
Metamorphoses. " Every minute's space "—so the
description runs—

> The streams with changed magic interlace:
> Sometimes like delicatest lattices,
> Cover'd with crystal vines; then weeping trees,
> Moving about as in a gentle wind,
> Which, in a wink, to watery gauze refin'd,
> Poured into shapes of curtain'd canopies,
> Spangled, and rich with liquid broideries
> Of flowers, peacocks, swans, and naiads fair.
> Swifter than lightning went these wonders are;
> And then the water, into stubborn streams
> Collecting, mimick'd the wrought oaken beams,
> Pillars and frieze, and high fantastic roof,
> Of those dusk places in times far aloof
> Cathedrals call'd.   (II. 613)

Ovid's
Metamor-
phoses.

" It was from Ovid's *Metamorphoses,*" says Colvin, " as
Englished by that excellent Jacobean translator, George
Sandys, that Keats, more than from any other source,
made himself familiar with the details of classic fable."[1]

---

[1] *Life of Keats,* p. 171.

Evidences of this are strewn freely over the pages of *Endymion*. The scene of the sleep of Adonis and the coming of Venus to awake him is drawn from the tenth book of the *Metamorphoses*; the description of Cybele (II. 639-649) is imitated from a passage in the same book where Venus is represented as telling to Adonis the story of Atalanta; the pursuit of Arethusa by Alpheus (II. 916) comes from the fifth book; and that of Glaucus and Scylla (Book III.) is given in the thirteenth and twenty-fourth books. This free use of Ovid, added to the emphasis which is laid throughout this passage on the alterations that are taking place in the form and significance of the magic fountains, leaves little room for doubt as to the meaning of the poet. He may have thought that in making use of the expressions " changed magic " (613) and " founts Protean " (627) he was giving a sufficiently broad hint of his purpose.

Bidding farewell to these sights Endymion passes Cybele. on and soon sees the vision of Cybele, to which allusion has already been made. Cybele, wife of Cronos and mother of the gods, may be taken to represent the fount and source of all these legends, in which the poet is now beginning to perceive a deeper meaning; and he has this brief glimpse of her shortly before his wanderings in the region of classical poetry are crowned with their great reward. For, at this point, he finds that the diamond path that he has been following ends abruptly in mid air. In his perplexity Endymion asks for divine help, and there comes to him a large eagle on which he flings himself and is borne down—

> Through unknown things; till exhaled asphodel
> And rose, with spicy fannings interbreath'd,
> Came swelling forth.   (II. 663)

The eagle lands him in the greenest nook of a jasmine bower all bestrown with golden moss. He wanders

through verdant cave and cell, and feels a swell of
sudden exaltation.   An intense longing for his heavenly
love comes upon him; he knows, however, that no
passionate striving of spirit will bring her to him, and
yielding quietly to the influences by which he feels himself to be surrounded, suddenly he finds that she is with
him.   Even now he does not realise the full measure of
the glory that is his, but the period of their intercourse
is more prolonged, more intimate, and more complete
than ever it has been before.

Diana.

This is the climax of the second book, and it is
evidently intended to set forth by means of picture and
imagery some part of the experience through which the
poet passed in the course of his efforts to attain to the
understanding of the innermost mysteries of poetry.
We may regard him as telling us, in the course of this
book, of some incident that awakened his interest in
classical poetry, and that led to his plunging into a deep
and thorough study of certain parts of it, more especially
the *Aeneid* of Virgil and the *Metamorphoses* of Ovid;
of the curiosity and interest which the study aroused in
him; of the discouragement that came upon him as he
reflected that this was the expression of the mind of an
age that had long passed away, whose aim in life and
mode of thought and manner of speech seemed to have
little or no meaning for the men and women of his day;
of the wonder and delight which he felt when, as by a
revelation, he became aware of a deeper and richer meaning that lay beneath the surface of these old myths and
legends; and then how he reached a point where it seemed
to him that classical poetry had done for him all that it
could do in the way of leading him to the ideal that he
was seeking.   It was at that time, when all the course
of painful striving through which he had gone seemed
to have led to no tangible result, that there came to him an

44

inspiration, as from some divine source, which carried him right into the very presence of the spirit of perfect poetry; and this mood of exaltation and attainment lasted longer and was more complete than ever before; and, though he knew, even while the mood was upon him, that it could not endure,[1] but would die away after a time, yet he felt cheered and encouraged, for he knew that he was coming nearer and nearer to the realisation of the full powers, the high ideal, towards which he was striving. This appears to be the meaning, so far as one has been able to trace it, that Keats intended to convey in this book, and, while we may feel that the climax is told in a manner not worthy of the loftiness of the experience that it is intended to represent, we must at the same time recognise that it reveals something of the earnestness and intensity with which Keats pursued his aims and ideals. The pleasure that comes from the exercise of the creative instinct is shared by many. The child who draws the picture of a cow or carves his little boat of bark knows something of it; the man who lays out a garden or designs a house, shares in it; the writer of verse that others can only read with a smile has felt some thrill of pleasure in the making of it; but which of us can hope to enter into the joy of the poet who has produced a masterpiece able to stir thousands of hearts by its subtle magic—

Our birth is but a sleep and a forgetting

or

Thou wast not born for death, immortal Bird!

This is the level of attainment, with the rapture that must belong to it, that Keats has attempted to depict for us in this book.

Endymion, awaking out of his great experience, finds that he is alone. He feels sad and forlorn, but no

---

[1] Ah, thou wilt steal
Away from me again, indeed. (II. 745)

longer resentful, as he had been on former occasions when these wonderful visitations had passed.   He sat down in a marvellous grotto and thought over the story of his life, and coming down to this latest experience he began to wonder what he still had to endure before he could come to the full realisation of his hopes.   As he pondered he heard a noise, and soon—

> On either side outgush'd, with misty spray,
> A copious spring; and both together dash'd
> Swift, mad, fantastic round the rocks.   (II. 918)

Alpheus and Arethusa.   It was Alpheus in pursuit of Arethusa.   She longs to yield, but fears the wrath of Diana; and Endymion, moved with a fellow feeling of pity for their longings unfulfilled, prays to his still unknown goddess to have compassion on them and to make them happy.   Then, turning, he moved along a sandy path and found that—

> The visions of the earth were gone and fled—
> He saw the giant sea above his head.   (II. 1022)

The significance of this incident, with which the second book closes, appears to be two-fold.   It is in the first place a fresh illustration of the life and power that may be found in these old stories for those who have sympathy and insight to enter into their spirit; and there is further, the suggestion, preparing the way for one aspect of what is to follow in the next book, that Endymion is coming to be less absorbed in his own perplexities and troubles, and is learning to look with a feeling of sympathy upon the difficulties of others; and this marks an important advance in the process of his training.

The introduction to the second book.   If we now turn to the lines that form the introduction to this book, we find that they bear out the interpretation to which the study of the rest of the book has led us. The essence of them is contained in the first seven lines,

46

and the remainder of the passage is merely expansion
and illustration of the one idea stated at the beginning :

> O sovereign power of love! O grief! O balm!
> All records, saving thine, come cool, and calm,
> And shadowy, through the mist of passed years :
> For others, good or bad, hatred and tears
> Have become indolent; but touching thine,
> One sigh doth echo, one poor sob doth pine,
> One kiss brings honey-dew from buried days.   (II. 1)

And he goes on to say that the tale of the wars around
Troy or of the campaigns of Alexander has little power
to move us, while our souls thrill with responsive
sympathy when we hear such stories as those of Troilus
and Cressida or of Imogen.   So, it will be remembered,
a large part of classical poetry is imaged as cold and
lifeless; its beauty is like that of the diamond or sapphire;
but where it enshrines the passion of love it pulsates with
life. Such stories as those of Venus and Adonis, or of the
river lovers, still retain their power to rouse our sympathy.

In working out the interpretation of this book it has More than the
experience of
been convenient to deal with it primarily as a record of Keats.
the personal experience of Keats; but here, no less than
in the first book, it is necessary to bear in mind that the
allegory has a wider significance, and is intended to
represent the process of training which may be regarded
as desirable, if not necessary, for anyone who aspires to
the name of poet.   It is evident that the journey of
Endymion suggests a much more extensive study of
classical literature than Keats ever had the opportunity
of carrying out.   He did, indeed, come to know Homer
with as much completeness as the translation of Chapman
made possible; he studied Ovid both with the help of
Sandys and in the original text; while, as noted above,
he translated the whole of the *Aeneid* for himself; but
beyond this his knowledge of the classics appears to have
been derived from such secondary sources as Tooke's

Pantheon, Lemprière's *Classical Dictionary* and Spence's *Polymetis*. He was fully conscious, however, of the disadvantages of the limited range of his own knowledge, and accordingly in describing Endymion's wanderings through the " dusky empire with its diadems " he suggests a much wider range of study, though the sketch is naturally coloured by reminiscences of what he knew best.

BOOK III.

The story of
Glaucus and
Scylla

The third book is mainly concerned with the story of Glaucus and Scylla. It tells how Glaucus, having won the power of living in the sea, saw and loved Scylla (399), and tried to win her, but, tiring of the pursuit, turned aside and yielded to the wiles of Circe (418). After a time he awoke to a sense of his degradation, and was condemned to impotence for a long space of time, while Scylla appeared to be dead (619). During this time he was witness of a shipwreck. One of the men from the ship, being carried by the sea towards Glaucus, thrust a scroll into his hand, but fell back and perished with the rest (674). On the scroll Glaucus found a message that gave him hope of deliverance. When Endymion in the course of his wanderings met Glaucus, the old man hailed him joyfully and claimed his help (234). By rightful use of the magic scroll Glaucus was restored to youthful energy and Scylla was revived (780), while those of the dead whose bodies had been carefully laid aside by Glaucus during the period of his punishment were restored to life, and all went in joyful procession to the hall of Neptune (868). There, after the singing of a hymn to the god, a vision of Oceanus was seen (994). Endymion fell senseless, but in his swoon received the promise of Diana that he should soon be raised to immortality. When he awoke he found himself in a cool forest beside a placid lake.

We have found that in the first book of this poem the underlying meaning, so far as one can trace it, appears to be concerned, in the earlier part of the book, with the new movement that made itself felt in the realm of English poetry from the middle of the eighteenth century; while in the latter part of the first and throughout the second book we are being told of the experiences through which a poet might pass as he came under the influence of such a movement and strove to realise its ideals in his own work. In the third book it seems that the more individual aspect of the story retires into the background for a time, and we are again chiefly concerned with the larger movements of English poetry. *represents a poetical movement.*

There is, as in the last book, an introductory passage of about forty lines, the significance of which may be more suitably considered when the meaning of the main theme of the book has been dealt with; but after this there is a further passage (to line 187) that intervenes before the story really moves on its way again, lines that are mainly devoted to praise of the beauty and influence of the moon. We are told of the gentle and far-reaching nature of this influence :

> Thou dost bless everywhere, with silver lip
> Kissing dead things to life . . . . .   (III. 56)
> . . . . thy benediction passeth not
> One obscure hiding place, one little spot
> Where pleasure may be sent.

Endymion's love for the moon

She is shining now, though with but a pale light, upon Endymion in his wanderings :

> thy cheek is pale
> For one whose cheek is pale : thou dost bewail
> His tears, who weeps for thee.   (III. 75)

49

But even these faint beams have power to warm the heart of Endymion, and to comfort him in his solitude. Endymion wonders at the power that she exercises; it had pervaded all the occupations of his earlier life, and as he grew up it still blended with all his ardours (160) *and for Diana.* Then his strange love came and the influence of the moon grew less.

> She came, and thou didst fade and fade away
> Yet not entirely! no, thy starry sway
> Has been an under-passion to this hour.   (III. 177)

He is torn between the attraction of the two:

> Dearest love, forgive
> That I can think away from thee and live!—
> Pardon me, airy planet, that I prize
> One thought beyond thine argent luxuries!   (III. 183)

and it is, of course, obvious that he does not recognise the identity of the two.

The meaning of the contrast. It can hardly be doubted, if we keep in view the general purpose of the poem, and the length at which this matter is treated, that we have here something of significance in relation to the work of the poet, some aspect of poetic theory that Keats felt to be of importance. It is, of course, true that Keats had been from childhood passionately fond of moonlight,[1] and this fact no doubt influenced the tone of the passage, and may, indeed, have given rise to it. But it says more than this, and one may find a clue to the further meaning in the repeated failure of Endymion to recognise the identity of his heavenly visitant with the moon whose beauty affected him so powerfully,[2] and starting with this as a guide we may

---

1 See Colvin, *Life of Keats*, pp. 166, 7.

2 This point occurs in each of the four books. When Endymion sees the vision for the first time he is watching the moon and is fascinated by her beauty (I. 591); she disappears behind a cloud (597) and then the goddess appears (602), but he does not connect the two. Again, before he begins his wanderings underground, the beauty of the moon fills him with delight and longing, but, so little is he conscious of her identity, that he begs her to point out his love's far dwelling (II. 178). In the fourth book the situation has grown even more complex because of the appearance of Diana in a new form, and the perplexity arising from his failure to perceive her identity is greater than ever.   (IV. 429, 438, 497; and cf. 95).

interpret the passage somewhat in this way. Cynthia (the moon) stands for that element in the attractiveness of poetry which depends upon beauty of form. It is, indeed, an influence as widespread as life itself; there is a rhythm in the growth of the flowers, in the song of the birds, in the movement of the rivers and the tides and it is, of course, a large part of the very essence of poetry. But poetry must also express feeling and passion though the moving power of passion will visit the poet less frequently, will be less constantly present as a force, than the gentler and milder influence of beauty in form. Yet, if the poet is to reach any high level of attainment, he must come to recognise that these two, different as their appearance may be, are not to be finally separated. When the poet, in moments of greatest achievement attains his ideal, he finds not merely that beauty of expression and beauty of feeling are both present, but that they can no longer be distinguished from one another; in the white heat of the finest inspiration he learns that they are one.[1]

Meanwhile Endymion has been wandering in the depths of ocean. He has passed many relics of former days—

> Old rusted anchors, helmets, breast-plates large　Ocean relics.
> Of gone sea-warriors ; brazen beaks and targe ;
> Rudders that for a hundred years had lost
> The sway of human hand :　(III. 123)

[1] Compare what Mr. A. C. Bradley says in his famous lecture, *Poetry for Poetry's Sake*: "The value of versification when it is indissolubly fused with meaning, can hardly be exaggerated. The gift for feeling it, even more, perhaps, than the gift for feeling the value of style, is the *specific* gift for poetry, as distinguished from other arts. But versification, taken as far as possible, all by itself, has a very different worth. Some aesthetic worth it has ; how much, you may experience by reading poetry in a language of which you do not understand a syllable. The pleasure is quite appreciable, but it is not great ; nor in actual poetic experience do you meet with it, as such, at all. For, I repeat, it is not *added* to the pleasure of the meaning when you read poetry that you do understand : by some mystery the music is then the music *of* the meaning, and the two are one." (*Oxford Lectures on Poetry*, p. 21.)

and these things give him a feeling of depression which is only removed by the soothing influence of the moon.

The passage based upon Shakespeare.

The passage, as is well known, is based upon the account given by Clarence of one part of his dream,[1] and Jeffrey's remark upon it is worth remembering—" It comes of no ignoble lineage, nor shames its high descent." This is well put, but it falls short of the truth, for in these lines Keats has rehandled the lines from Shakespeare with so much skill and imaginative power that they surpass the material of which they were built.   But for our present purpose it is more to the point to see if we can define the character of the changes that Keats has introduced, for in this way we have the best hope of getting upon the track of his purpose.   It will be seen on comparing the two passages that Keats has throughout laid stress on the antiquity of the remains which Endymion found on the sea bottom, while Shakespeare does not refer at all to this aspect of them.   Thus the " great anchors " of Clarence's dream become " old rusted anchors;" " wedges of gold " are transformed into " gold vase emboss'd with long-forgotten story "; and several things not found in the earlier passage, such as the " mouldering scrolls, writ in the tongue of heaven, by those souls who first were on the earth," are introduced, all emphasizing the same point.   Some men would have

---

[1] Methought I saw a thousand fearful wrecks;
Ten thousand men that fishes gnaw'd upon;
Wedges of gold, great anchors, heaps of pearl,
Inestimable stones, unvalued jewels,
All scatter'd in the bottom of the sea:
Some lay in dead men's skulls, and, in those holes
Where eyes did once inhabit, there were crept,
As 'twere in scorn of eyes, reflecting gems,
Which woo'd the slimy bottom of the deep,
And mock'd the dead bones that lay scatter'd by.
(*King Richard the Third*, I. 4.)

delighted to examine these relics, but it was not so with Endymion :

A cold leaden awe
These secrets struck into him ; and unless
Diana had chas'd away that heaviness
He might have died.   (III. 136)

What Keats appears to have in mind is that the study of old things merely because they are old is not an inspiring pursuit for a poet.   Antiquarianism, as he may have met with in the pages of Strutt or of Ritson, only depresses the spirit of poetry, and may even kill it if a higher inspiration does not come to keep it alive.   That Keats did not undervalue the imaginative treatment of stories of olden days is abundantly clear, but for one who could do this with the genius of Scott there were scores who would be dull and wearisome, and the poet hurried from them to seek fresh inspiration elsewhere.

At length as he lifted up his eyes,

He saw, far in the concave green of the sea,
An old man sitting calm and peacefully.   (III. 191)

Glaucus.

This was Glaucus, whose story fills the greater part of this book, for though Endymion plays an important part in the development of events, the interest attaching to his actions is for the time subordinate, while Glaucus and his past history take the most prominent place.

The story of Glaucus, as he told it to Endymion His story. (III. 318 sq.) offers in its early stages some points of similarity to that of Endymion himself.   He was a fisherman, and he delighted in his life upon the sea. He felt the same craving as Endymion had felt for quietness and meditation and communion with Nature :

the crown
Of all my life was utmost quietude :
More did I love to lie in cavern rude,
Keeping in wait whole days for Neptune's voice,
And if it came at last, hark, and rejoice ! (III. 352)

53

And he so far achieved his desire that he found himself able to live and move freely in the depths of the ocean.

Its meaning. It is not until we reach a later part of the story of Glaucus that we meet with any very clear indications of its allegorical meaning, but it may be worth while to point out at once what appears to be the true line of interpretation, making use by anticipation of clues that will be found further on.

The story of Endymion as we have seen, represents in one aspect the growth of the new spirit which was making itself felt in English poetry before the time of Keats, and which found its fulfilment in what we know as the New Romantic Movement. It is this more general side of his theme that the poet appears to be dealing with in the third book, the more individual and personal aspect of it being dropped for the time.

A new poetic movement. Just as Endymion represents the poetic spirit which was animating the age of Keats, so Glaucus in his youth, may be regarded as representing a different poetic spirit, animating an earlier age.[1] His loneliness, his longing for utmost quietude, his desire to be free of Neptune's Kingdom (III. 377), his entrance into this new life, his passion for and pursuit of Scylla—all these early experiences, corresponding largely to those through which Endymion passed, represent the yearnings, the idealisms and the tentative efforts which belong to the development of a new movement, and, while the details vary, the general course that it follows is much the same in one age as in another. Such a movement, for example, was that which had for its aim the attainment of correctness of style and polish of form in the days of Waller and his contemporaries, and those who kept that

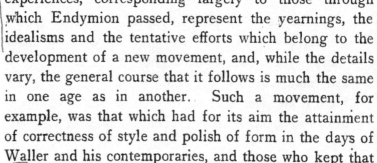

1 It does not appear necessary to take the thousand years (326) in a literal sense.

ideal before them no doubt strove with no less earnestness and sincerity to reach it than the poets of a later age strove after the different ideals that seemed to them so much loftier.   We are told clearly about the earnestness and eagerness of the pursuit:

> My passion grew
> The more, the more I saw her dainty hue
> Gleam delicately through the azure clear,
> Until 'twas too fierce agony to bear.   (III. 407)

But from this point his story ceases to resemble that of The failure. Endymion, for, impatient at his want of success in attaining his ideal, Glaucus turned aside to seek help from Circe, and under the influence of her baleful charms allowed himself to be seduced from his aim, to forget his high ideal, and to follow an unworthy and degrading course of life.   After a time he came to himself and saw in her true light the witch to whose charms he had surrendered.   He watched her as she exercised her evil influence upon those around her—

> Wizard and brute,
> Laughing, and wailing, grovelling, serpentining,
> Showing tooth, tusk, and venom-bag, and sting!
> O such deformities!   (III. 500)

until he was filled with remorse.   But it was too late; he had incurred the fierce displeasure of the goddess and was condemned to an age-long decrepitude.   He plunged once more into the ocean, only to discover that Scylla was dead, slain by the hated power of Circe, and as for himself it was not long before his

> limbs became
> Gaunt, wither'd, sapless, feeble, cramp'd and lame.
> (III. 637)

If we now attempt to follow up the clue which has guided us thus far it would appear that we must look for some critical phase in the development of English poetry where, in the view of Keats, things took a disastrous course; where poetry turned aside from its nobler aims, became unfaithful to its lofty ideals, and, falling under influences which, though superficially attractive, were essentially mean and base, was reduced to a state of decrepitude. And it is not difficult to put one's finger upon the period when, in the opinon of Keats, a change of this nature had come over English poetry. He regarded the spirit that became dominant after the Restoration as a spirit of unfaithfulness to the true ideals of poetry. " He hated," says Sir Sidney Colvin, " the whole ' Augustan ' and post-Augustan tribe of social and moral essayists in verse, and Pope their illustrious master, most of all."[1] His feeling was, of course, shared by other poets of the time. There is a passage in an essay of Wordsworth's[2] which had appeared not long before Keats began to write *Endymion*, in which Pope and his school are described in terms that Keats would have heartily endorsed, and one may almost suspect that the younger poet is merely translating into the picturesque imagery of his poem what the elder one has expressed in direct criticism. The passage reads as follows :

Wordsworth on Pope.

" The arts by which Pope, soon afterwards, contrived to procure to himself a more general and a higher reputation than perhaps any English Poet ever attained during his lifetime, are known to the judicious. And as well known is it to them that the undue exertion of these arts is the cause why Pope has for some time held a rank in literature, from which, if he had not been seduced by an over-love of immediate popularity, and had confided more in his native genius, he never could have descended. He bewitched the nation by his melody, and dazzled it by his polished style, and was

---

1 *Life of Keats*, p. 18.

2 Essay supplementary to the Preface to the 1815 edition of Wordsworth's poems: reprinted in the Prose Works of William Wordsworth, Vol. II. (ed. Knight). The passage quoted is on page 238.

himself blinded by his own success.   Having wandered
from humanity in his Eclogues with boyish inexperience,
the praise, which these compositions obtained, tempted
him into the belief that Nature was not to be trusted, at
least in pastoral Poetry.   To prove this by example he
put his friend Gay upon writing those Eclogues which
the author intended to be burlesque.   The instigator of
the work, and his admirers, could perceive in them nothing
but what was ridiculous.   Nevertheless, though these
Poems contain some detestable passages, the effect, as
Dr. Johnson well observes, " of reality and truth become
conspicuous, even when the intention was to show them
grovelling and degraded."

In *Sleep and Poetry*, which had appeared only a
few months before Keats wrote the passage now under
consideration,[1] he had expressed his feelings on this
matter in no uncertain way.   After speaking with Keats on the classical school
enthusiasm of the work of the poets of the Elizabethan
age, when " the Muses were well nigh cloyed with
honours," he goes on to ask—

> " Could all this be forgotten? "

and the answer is,

> Yes, a schism
> Nurtured by foppery and barbarism,
> Made great Apollo blush for this his land.

He speaks of them as " dead to things they knew not
of," and finally denounces them as an

> Ill-fated, impious race!
> That blasphemed the bright Lyrist to his face,
> And did not know it,—no, they went about
> Holding a poor, decrepid standard out
> Mark'd with most flimsy mottos, and in large
> The name of one Boileau !   (ll. 181, sq.)

The very expressions of which Keats makes use in this
passage suggest in a striking way its relation with this

---

1 The volume which includes *Sleep and Poetry* was published in March,
    1817.   The third book of *Endymion* was written in September of
    the same year.

part of the story of Glaucus.   While under the spell
of Circe he was " dead " to the beauty of Scylla; he had
been guilty of " impiety " in deserting the nobler ideal
for the baser; he was certainly " ill-fated," and the word
" decrepid " would apply more exactly to him as
described in the story than to the standard of the school
of Pope.

We may take it then that Keats is in this passage
describing to us in picturesque form what he regarded
as the tragical history of English poetry after the
Restoration.   He shows us how it was ready for a fresh
adventure, and how, when a new and beautiful ideal was
in sight, it had allowed itself to be turned aside from its
high aims, and had abandoned itself to the pursuit of
false pleasures—a course that resulted in a long period
of hopeless futility: the ideal had to all appearance
perished.   Such was certainly his view of the course
of poetry in that period, and it would appear that this
is the real meaning of the story of Glaucus.

What Circe stands for. It seems, indeed, that Keats, not content with drawing this unflattering picture of the general tendency and
influence of the school of poetry for which he felt such
a hearty dislike, has in the figure of Circe sketched a
portrait—or perhaps one should say a caricature—of no
less a person than its distinguished head and chief, Pope
himself.   This is suggested by certain resemblances
between the expressions which Wordsworth applies to
Pope in the passage quoted above and the account of
Circe in the poem;[1] it is confirmed by the description of
those who surrounded Circe as

> Shewing tooth, tusk, and venom-bag, and sting!
> (IJ[502)

[1] Note, for instance, " The arts by which Pope contrived   .   .   " :
" the undue exertion of these arts: " and compare what is said of
Gay's Eclogues—" The instigator of the work (Pope)   .   .   . .
could perceive in them nothing but what was ridiculous," with
line 509, " Oft-times upon the sudden she laughed out."

words that aptly represent the tribe of petty and malicious
satirists that basked in the sunshine of Pope's favours,
or more often writhed under his lash.   But the passage
that appears to leave little, if any, room for doubt as to
the intention of Keats occurs a little further down in the
description of the same incident :

> Avenging, slow,
> Anon she took a branch of mistletoe,
> And emptied on't a black dull-gurgling phial :
> Groan'd one and all, as if some piercing trial
> Was sharpening for their pitiable bones.
> She lifted up the charm : appealing groans
> From their poor breasts went sueing to her ear
> In vain ; remorseless as an infant's bier
> She whisk'd against their eyes the sooty oil.
> Whereat was heard a noise of painful toil,
> Increasing gradual to a tempest rage,
> Shrieks, yells and groans of torture-pilgrimage ;
> Until their grieved bodies 'gan to bloat
> And puff from the tail's end to stifled throat :
> Then was appalling silence : then a sight
> More wildering than all that hoarse affright ;
> For the whole herd, as by a whirlwind writhen,
> Went through the dismal air like one huge Python
> Antagonizing Boreas,—and so vanish'd.
> Yet there was not a breath of wind : she banish'd
> These phantoms with a nod.   (III. 513)

One can hardly fail to recognise in these lines a The Dunciad.
picture, drawn with no small degree of humour and skill,
of the treatment meted out by Pope to the petty scribblers
of his day in the pages of *The Dunciad*.   The merciless
spirit in which the punishment was administered, the
" shrieks and yells and groans " that it produced, and
the entire disappearance of the victims from the literary
stage are excellently depicted : Horneck, Roome, Jacob,
Goode—who would ever hear their names to-day unless
he reads the lines in which they received their castiga-
tion?   Pope, indeed, " banished these phantoms with
a nod."

The words " Avenging, slow," with which the passage referring to *The Dunciad* opens, may or may not

59

have been chosen with reference to that poem, but they apply to it more exactly than they do to the Circe of classical legend. In the preface to the first edition (1728), Pope indicates that his purpose is to avenge himself upon his enemies: " I will only observe as a fact that every week for these two months past, the town has been persecuted with pamphlets, advertisements, letters, and weekly essays, not only against the wit and writings, but against the character and person of Mr. Pope: " while as for the " slowness," the same preface speaks of it as having been " the labour of full six years of his life."

The story of the rescued scroll.

An incident that is related a little further on in the story of Glaucus appears to carry a meaning that confirms the line of interpretation that has been given to the preceding part of the poem. After Glaucus had passed a long time in the state of decrepitude to which he had been reduced by Circe, he was one day sitting on a rock that stood out above the spray when he saw a vessel approach. A storm arose, the vessel was wrecked before his eyes; the feebleness to which he had been reduced made of no avail his eager desire to save those who were drowning, and he saw one after another sink helpless into the deep. While he was still watching there emerged from the waves an old man's hand, holding out a scroll and a wand. Glaucus seized these treasures and even touched the hand that held them, but it slipped from his grasp and sank. The storm abated and the sun shone again.

> I was athirst
> To search the book, and in the warming air
> Parted its dripping leaves with eager care.
> Strange matters did it treat of, and drew on
> My soul page after page, till well-nigh won
> Into forgetfulness: (III. 676)

and, above all, he found to his great joy that the book contained the promise of his ultimate deliverance, for

it spoke of a youth, " by heavenly power lov'd and led,"
who should stand before him and who was to be told how
to bring about the redemption of Glaucus from the
punishment to which he had been condemned; and it was
added,

> The youth elect
> Must do the thing, or both will be destroy'd.   (III. 710)

To interpret rightly the significance of this incident A redeeming influence.
in relation to the meaning of the book as a whole we
must look for some influence that gave promise of new
life to English poetry after the period of decrepitude
which was the penalty of yielding to the influence of
Pope.   It may be well to note in passing that we are not
concerned with the justice or injustice of such a method
of representing this school of poetry.   Whether it is
to be regarded as a fair, though severe satire, or an unfair
caricature, is a matter outside our present enquiry.
There is no doubt as to the views of Keats on the point,
and the interpretation here suggested corresponds with
those views.   It is, however, generally agreed that the
influences which brought about a change of spirit in
English poetry are represented most completely in the
revival of interest in the ballad, and that Bishop Percy's
Reliques of Ancient English Poetry at once expressed
and stimulated this interest in the most effective manner.
Wordsworth, in the essay to which reference has already
been made, speaks with great enthusiasm of Percy's work,
and, after pointing out the influence that it had exerted
on the revival of poetry in Germany, adds : *For our own
country, its Poetry has been absolutely redeemed by it.*"[1]

1 Prose works of William Wordsworth (ed. Knight), Vol. II., p. 247,
   The italics are ours.   It is worth noting that in September, 1817,
   when Keats was writing this third book of *Endymion*, he was
   staying at Oxford with his friend Bailey, and his letters record
   that they had been reading Wordsworth together.   See Letter
   to Reynolds, 21st September, 1817.   In a letter written to Bailey
   a little later (November, 1817) he refers again to Wordsworth.

The correspondence between this expression of Wordsworth's and the story as shaped by Keats is so striking that one can hardly suppose it to be accidental, especially when taken in conjunction with the parallelism previously noted between essay and poem; and it is not unlikely that in this sentence we have the germ out of which the incident originally grew in the mind of Keats.

The history of the ballads. When we come to examine the details of the incident their correspondence with the history of the ballads becomes evident. He tells us, in words which seem carefully adapted to the meaning underlying the surface that

The crew had gone,
By one and one, to pale oblivion;   (III. 665)

and even the one whose hand, emerging, held up the scroll that Glaucus safely grasped, was not himself rescued, but sank again and disappeared. This corresponds exactly with the fate that has overtaken the makers of the ballads; some fragments of their work have been rescued from destruction, but they themselves have all sunk down into oblivion. Not even their names have survived, nor is it known who gathered together the ballads that Percy found in the famous scroll that he rescued only by a hairsbreadth from destruction. Yet, if only the lovers of poetry had stirred themselves earlier how much more might have been rescued. " It was not till the publication of Allan Ramsay's *Evergreen* and *Tea Table Miscellany*, and of Bishop Percy's *Reliques* (1765)," says Mr. Andrew Lang, " that a serious effort was made to recover Scottish and English folksongs from the recitation of the old people who still knew them by heart." And when we ask why the effort was not made earlier, the answer that Keats puts forward is that it was due to the paralysing effect of the influence of the school of Pope :

> O they had all been sav'd but crazed eld
> Annull'd my vigorous cravings : and thus quell'd
> And curb'd, think on't, O Latmian! did I sit
> Writhing with pity, and a cursing fit
> Against that hell-born Circe.   (III. 661)

The interest that they roused is described in the lines already quoted (p. 60) and the story goes on to tell of the promise of redemption that was contained in the scroll, and of how this promise was fulfilled when Endymion, representing the spirit of the new poetry, scattered first upon Glaucus, and then upon Scylla, some of the " powerful fragments " of the rescued scroll, and how under its magic influence Glaucus was restored to his youthful vigour and beauty, and Scylla came to life again. Underneath the symbolism we can hardly fail to recognise that Keats is representing to us the restoration of a true poetic ideal, and the infusion of fresh life and energy into poetry after its long period of futile decrepitude, and that he is emphasising the part played by the rediscovery of the ballads in bringing about this renaissance.   The other details of the story—the undoing of the tangled thread, the thread which was so weak for Glaucus, but which Endymion handled safely; the reading of the shell on which Glaucus could see " no sign or character "; the breaking of the wand against the lyre, which was followed by some sweet and sudden music— all these are significant in different ways of the magic power immanent in the spirit of the new poetry.

It will be remembered that the same message that gave to Glaucus the hope of ultimate redemption spoke of a task that he must undertake during the period of his bondage : The task of Glaucus.

> all lovers tempest-tost,
> And in the savage overwhelming lost,
> He shall deposit side by side, until
> Time's creeping shall the dreary space fulfil.   (III. 703)

63

This may be taken to represent the reverent regard that was paid to the great poets of former times even during the period of poetical decrepitude. There is no lack of evidence on this point. Dryden, in his *Preface to the Fables*, for example, makes a comparison between Chaucer and Ovid which works out on the whole to the advantage of the English poet; the imitation of Spenser, sometimes in form only, at other times in a way that shows a feeling for the magic beauty of his poetry, was a frequent occupation among the minor, and an occasional amusement of the major poets of this time;[1] while Johnson's *Lives of the Poets* and Thomas Warton's *Observations on the Faerie Queene*, which appeared only nine years after the death of Pope, illustrate the same feeling. The spirit that had animated these poets was no longer a vital force in English poetry, but the care that was taken of them was a hopeful sign for the future. When Endymion came to them he found their

patient lips
All ruddy,—for here death no blossom nips   (III. 739)

That is to say, their poetry remained unspoiled, even though for the time they could not be said to exercise any living influence. But now, after renewing the youthful vigour of Glaucus and Scylla, Endymion passed on—

Showering those powerful fragments on the dead.
And, as he pass'd, each lifted up his head,
As doth a flower at Apollo's touch.   (III. 784)

The revival of interest in poetry which resulted from the study of the ballads spread to the works of the older poets, so that they began once more to take their place

[1] Professor Phelps has an interesting chapter on this matter in *The Beginnings of the English Romantic Movement* (Ginn), and in an Appendix gives a list of fifty-seven imitations of Spenser published between 1706 and 1775.

among the vital influences of the day.   The music of
poetry was once more heard in the land :

> Delicious symphonies, like airy flowers,
> Budded, and swell'd, and, full-blown, shed full showers
> Of light, soft, unseen leaves of sounds divine.   (III. 798)

As the host of those who had been redeemed by this The other host
magic power moved on their way to the palace of Neptune

> they saw descending thick
> Another multitude.   Whereat more quick
> Moved either host.   (III. 820)

This is probably intended to refer to the romantic movement on the continent of Europe, more particularly in
France and Germany, which developed side by side with
the movement in England, and to the way in which each
movement stimulated the other.

The closing part of the book describes the joyous The festival in Neptune's palace.
celebration of this fresh renaissance held in the palace
of Neptune, symbolical of the enthusiasm and delight
that were aroused by the revived interest in the poetry
of past ages.   The general bearing of the passage seems
sufficiently clear, but there are two incidents in it that
require a little closer examination.

The first of these is the appearance at the festival
of a number of the more ancient gods :

> On oozy throne
> Smooth-moving came Oceanus the old,   Oceanus.
> To take a latest glimpse at his sheep-fold,
> Before he went into his quiet cave
> To muse for ever :   (III. 993)

and with him came Doris and Nereus and Amphion (an
error for Arion) and others.

We cannot but call to mind the passage in the second
book (639 sq.) where Endymion comes upon the vision
of Cybele in the course of his wanderings underground.
In both cases Keats appears to be suggesting that the
spirit of poetry, as it found expression in the earliest

65

efforts of mankind, is looking with benevolent regard upon this latest manifestation, differing greatly in form and expression, yet animated by the same spirit of reverence, and fostered by the same divine protection as in former ages.

The second tells of the swoon into which Endymion fell after looking upon this vision of the elder gods:

> The palace whirls
> Around giddy Endymion; seeing he
> Was there far strayed from mortality.   (III. 1005)

He fell unconscious at the feet of Neptune, and was carried away by the Nereids.

It can hardly be doubted that some distinct meaning underlies this incident, and, keeping a firm hold of the clue by which we have been guided thus far we may arrive at a reasonable interpretation of it.   The salient points that must be kept in view are, that it is Endymion who has played a leading part in the revival of the dead forms of those who had been tended by the care of Glaucus, and yet, when the revival is complete, and is the occasion of great rejoicing, Endymion alone is unable to bear it, and sinks into unconsciousness notwithstanding the assurances that he has received of an early fulfilment of his desires.   Bearing in mind that Endymion stands for the spirit of the new poetry, we may recognise, as has already been pointed out, that we have here sketched for us the way in which this spirit brought renewed life and significance into the study of the earlier poets.   They had never ceased to be regarded with respect and admiration, but under the new influence they came to have a fresh vitality that was a source of delight and an occasion for thanksgiving.

So far the path is fairly plain.   And though the next stretch of it is less clearly marked, we are probably following the right track if we interpret the remaining

66

part of the story as showing that although the spirit of the new poetry has reacted thus powerfully on the older poetry, it cannot live upon the result of this.   There is hope and promise that its ideals may be fulfilled, but for the moment the very success that it has achieved in giving new life and meaning to the poetry of earlier days may tend to lessen its own vitality.   Certainly it cannot flourish upon inspiration drawn merely from its pre-decessors.   In seeking them it has strayed too far from mortality.   It can only become a living force by seeking contact with the actual life of men and women, and by entering into their joys and sorrows.   The way in which this is accomplished and the ideal finally reached will be found in the next book.

The lines that form the introduction to this book are The introduction to the third book. not in Keats's happiest vein; nor do they at first sight appear to have much bearing on the main theme of the poem.   Their most obvious reference is political, and in this sense they denounce the empty pomp of incom-petent rulers who have induced submissive peoples to receive them with mistaken enthusiasm. But an examina-tion of the phrases used makes it evident that they may bear another meaning, and, indeed, appear to have been chosen for that purpose.   We may question the poetic fitness of such expressions as " most prevailing tinsel," or " baaing vanities," but there can be no doubt that they effectively describe the feeling that Keats entertained for the writings of Pope and his school.   He regarded them as showing " not one tinge of sanctuary splen-dour; " that is to say, they had never offered Milton's prayer that he might be

From out His secret altar touched with sacred fire :

and he may well have been thinking more of them than

67

of those who had incurred Leigh Hunt's political
animosity when he wrote :

> With unladen breasts,
> Save of blown self-applause, they proudly mount
> To their spirit's perch, their being's high account,
> Their tiptop nothings, their dull skies, their thrones.
>
> (III. 12)

The contrast that he proceeds to draw describes no less
clearly his feeling as to the loftier aims and ideals of
the poetical movement in the midst of which he was living
when compared with those of the previous age :

> No, there are throned seats unscalable
> But by a patient wing, a constant spell,
> Or by ethereal things that, unconfin'd,
> Can make a ladder of the eternal wind,
> And poise about in cloudy thunder-tents
> To watch the abysm-birth of elements.   (III. 23)

A careful reading of the whole passage makes it evident
that while the political meaning is on the surface, the
literary is clearly to be seen just underneath it.   Moreover, while the political reference has no recognisable
bearing on the matters with which the poem is concerned,
the literary significance of the passage brings it into
immediate relation with the meaning which we have found
to underlie the story of this book.

BOOK IV.

The story.   The story of the fourth book turns upon one strong
situation which is presented with some degree of power.
The situation arises from a new and irresistible attraction
that Endymion feels for an Indian maiden who now
appears for the first time.   After his sea adventures he
finds himself in a green forest near a placid lake and
there he hears a plaintive cry (40), which, as he discovers,
comes from a beautiful Indian maiden who has failed

to find solace in the revelry of Bacchus (268) and is longing for human affection. He is torn between the attraction that he feels for her, and his devotion to his heavenly love. The development of the situation thus presented is less effective, and one cannot but feel that the story has suffered for the sake of the allegory. Mercury comes down, and at a touch of his wand there spring from the earth two jet-black winged steeds on which Endymion and the maiden fly up into the regions of the sky (347). There, overcome by slumber, he dreams that he is in heaven, and wakes to find himself indeed in the presence of his divine love (436). In sore perplexity he turns, now to her, now to the Indian maid, and yet in spite of all appearance he knows in his heart that he is not unfaithful to either. At length he finds that his companion has vanished, and soon afterwards her steed plunges down to the earth (512). Endymion's steed bears him to the Cave of Quietude, where he fails to see the guests passing on their way to Diana's wedding feast, though he seems to have heard their song (556, 611).

His steed brings him down to earth again, and there he finds his Indian love (623). Now that he feels his feet once more planted on solid ground he determines to devote himself to this earthly, human love, feeling that he has been too presumptuous in aspiring to a heavenly destiny. To Endymion's dismay she tells him that she is forbidden to accept his love (752). He sits despondent on the very spot where he had first seen the vision of Diana, and while he sits there Peona appears (800). She sees his downcast look, and bids him be happy, for she will rejoice that he has found such a lovely mate. He declares that he will live a hermit's life, and that Peona alone shall visit him, but expresses a hope that the Indian maid will stay with Peona (870). He bids farewell to them both, and they leave him, but he calls them back, begging them to meet him once more that evening in the grove behind great Diana's temple (911). The denouement forms an effective close to the story. As the sun sinks Endymion makes his way to the temple, thinking that surely his troubles and his life must now have an ending. The two maidens are there, but, as he utters his desire that heaven's will may be declared, a wonderful change takes place. His Indian love is transformed, and he sees that she is no other than his divine love, Cynthia or Diana. They bid farewell to Peona with a promise that she should meet them many a time in these forests, and they vanish.

> Peona went
> Home through the gloomy wood in wonderment.

Its meaning.

We have now to consider the meaning of this closing part of the story and its relation to the allegory as we have thus far traced it.[1]

The cry of the Indian maiden.

The cry of the Indian maiden, with which the story resumes its way, represents the cry that is always going up from humanity in all quarters of the world for sympathy and help. To Endymion this was a new and unexpected appeal and yet it is one to which his heart instinctively responded. So, Keats would tell us, in the development of the soul of the poet as he knew it, the ambition to excel in poetry first took possession of him, and it was only after he had been pursuing this aim for a considerable time that a new desire began to appeal to him, the desire of doing something to serve his fellow men. This was not a new conception for Keats. In

---

1 In his edition of the Poems of Keats (Methuen, 1907), Professor de Sélincourt has given a more detailed explanation of the allegory as developed in the fourth book than has elsewhere been attempted. Although the line of treatment here followed differs in some respects from that which he has adopted, I wish to record with gratitude my obligation to his interpretation, which has been of more service than anything else that I have seen in opening up the way to a fuller understanding of the allegory

Sleep and Poetry, which had appeared in the volume
published in March, 1817, he outlines the same order of
development :

> O for ten years, that I may overwhelm
> Myself in poesy; so may I do the deed
> That my own soul has to itself decreed.

And after sketching symbolically the way in which he
would spend this period of training, he goes on to say :

> And can I ever bid these joys farewell?
> Yes, I must pass them for a nobler life,
> Where I may find the agonies, the strife
> Of human hearts.

But a new element is introduced into the later treatment
of the idea, that of the clash between the two ideals, and
the doubt and perplexity of mind that is the consequence
of this clash. So keenly did Endymion realise the
trouble of the Indian maid, and so fully did his heart
respond to her appeal, that he felt perplexed and troubled
beyond endurance. He loved his mysterious goddess The conflict
no less than before; his intense delight in the beauty of
the moon was as great as ever; and these two had already
appeared to him to be in strange conflict,[1] for he had not
recognised them as two phases of one devotion; and now,
to add to his perplexity, he felt himself drawn by an
irresistible attraction to the Indian maiden, to whose tale
of sorrow he had listened. " I have a triple soul!" he
cried, torn by this painful conflict of feeling. Such,
Keats would have us understand, is the trouble and perplexity in the mind of the poet while he looks upon beauty
of form and intensity of feeling in poetry as separate and
conflicting ideals, more especially when their rivalry is
complicated by a larger desire to do some service of real
value to mankind.

[1] Book III., lines 175-187 : see page 50.

To Endymion it seems at the moment that he cannot but yield to the cry for sympathy and help, sacrificing all his former hopes and ideals, though such a sacrifice must bring death as a consequence:

> Thou art my executioner, and I feel
> Loving and hatred, misery and weal,
> Will in a few short hours be nothing to me,
> And all my story that much passion slew me.   (IV. 111.)

But the maiden does not see that Endymion's love for her need bring any such dire consequences in its train. Leaving this doubt unsolved Endymion asks her about her former life, and in response she sings a song—one of the most beautiful things in the whole poem—telling of the mystery and the inevitability of sorrow in human life. She goes on to speak of her unsatisfied longing for sympathy:

The song of sorrow.

> in the whole world wide
> There was no one to ask me why I wept.   (IV. 183)

And then telling the story that is always being repeated in the history of the race, she relates how she tried to find satisfaction in the pursuit of pleasure:

> And as I sat, over the light blue hills
> There came a noise of revellers: the rills
> Into the wide stream came of purple hue—
>   'Twas Bacchus and his crew!   (IV. 193)

They called her to join them:

> Come hither, lady fair, and joined be
>   To our wild minstrelsy!   (IV. 226)

She followed at their invitation, and through every clime watched humanity yielding to the call of pleasure; but it was of no avail:

> Into these regions came I following him,
> Sick hearted, weary—so I took a whim
> To stray away into these forests drear
>   Alone, without a peer:
> And I have told thee all thou mayest hear.   (IV. 268)

And she takes up again the song with which she began :

> Come then, Sorrow!
> Sweetest Sorrow!
> Like an own babe I nurse thee on my breast:
> I thought to leave thee
> And deceive thee,
> But now of all the world I love thee best. (IV. 279)

It seems strange that after such a surpassingly beautiful rendering of one aspect of his theme Keats should have allowed himself to lapse immediately into a strain of weak and maudlin sentiment that for the moment excuses the worst severity of his critics, but so it is.   The lines in which Endymion declares his devotion to the maiden fall as far below the normal level of the poem as did the former passage in which he expressed his passion for the unknown goddess. , We feel inclined to adopt the lines that follow and to apply them to this part of the poem : to cry a triple woe that such

An unfortunate passage

> words went echoing dismally
> Through the wide forest—a most fearful tone. (IV. 321)

But it is not difficult to recognise the intention that under-lies the passage; and this is no less true and cogent than the expression of it is false and deplorable.   Keats is trying to show with what irresistible force the passion for humanity may lay hold of a man when his ears and heart are open to its sorrows, and how he is impelled to put aside all other claims in order to devote himself wholly to this one service.   A no less passionate devotion had filled the soul of Endymion when his mysterious goddess had last visited him (III. 739-761), and, though we may well wish that both passages had been written in a manner more worthy of the genius that sustained Keats through so much of his work, we cannot but recognise that the parallelism in itself adds a true significance to the poem.

with a true meaning.

73

While Endymion was pouring out his protestations
of love a voice was heard crying *Woe! Woe! Woe to that
Endymion!* One can find little or no help in this place
towards the explanation of this incident, but if we compare with it a later passage (632 sq.), where Endymion
again declares his readiness to sacrifice everything in
order to devote himself exclusively to the new-found love,
we may gain some light on its meaning. In each case he is
checked; in this instance by the cry of woe, in the later
one by the refusal of the maiden : " I may not be thy
love " (752). The intention in each case probably is to
suggest that if the poet in his passion for humanity
abandons his poetic ideals he is committing a grave error
which cannot result in good.

At this point in the story Mercury appears and
touches the earth with his wand. From it there spring
two winged steeds. They evidently have a meaning
similar to that of the chariot in *Sleep and Poetry* : they
represent the power of the imagination. It may be noted
that just as the chariot in the earlier poem appears immediately after the recognition by the poet of the necessity
of entering into " the agonies, the strife of human hearts,"
so in this case it is when he is distracted by the conflict of
his feelings, and is shuddering at the cry of woe, that the
intervention of Mercury takes place. Trusting himself
to this new power Endymion and his companion are
carried aloft, far above the level of the earth.

It is worth while turning back for a moment to note
how this readiness of Endymion to commit himself to
the guidance of what he felt to be a higher power, offering
to lead him, is repeatedly illustrated in the course of the
poem. It is suggested in each of the three original
appearances; in the quickness with which he saw that
some divine power was manifesting itself in the magic bed
of flowers (I. 559), in his readiness to follow the cloudy

74

Cupid flying above the well (᷈ 891); and again in his listening attitude before the voice called to him from the cave; and the eagerness with which he hurried in when he heard it (I. 960). But it is shown more clearly as the story proceeds. When the golden butterfly came out of the flower he followed it with enthusiasm till it vanished (II. 66), and then when further direction was given to him he did not " contend one moment in reflection " (II. 215), but " fled into the fearful deep." There when the path that he was following ended " abrupt in middle air " (II. 653) he threw himself " without one impious word " (II. 659) upon the eagle that " crost towards him," trusting himself unhesitatingly to this divine messenger and caring not how perilous the adventure might seem. It was a similar instinct that led him to respond to the appeal of Glaucus for help (III. 282, 712) and to listen to the cry of the Indian maid; and, as we shall see, the consummation is reached when Endymion explicitly declares himself ready to submit entirely to the will of heaven (IV. 974).

In all these instances Keats is showing us, by his usual method of concrete images, what he regards as the real meaning of poetic inspiration. There is the impulse or suggestion that appears to come from some source outside of the poet himself, but, if any result is to follow, there must also be, on the part of the poet, a quickness to perceive and a readiness to respond to the promptings that come to him. It is, of course, a truth of wider application than that which is given to it here, but this is the aspect of it that belongs to the theme of the poem, and the repeated reference to the idea suggests how much value Keats placed upon it. It was a similar idea that he had pictured in *Sleep and Poetry* when he represented the charioteer (the poet) as coming down in his car (the imagination) and, while there pass before him " shapes

75

of delight and mystery and fear," he leans forward " most awfully intent," and seems to listen, and writes " with hurrying glow." It is the poet acting as the channel through which the divine can speak to humanity. In a letter written to Haydon soon after he had begun to work at this poem Keats gives expression to a similar feeling : " Thank God ! I do begin arduously where I leave off, notwithstanding occasional depressions; and I hope for the support of a High Power while I climb this little eminence [*Endymion*], and especially in my Years of more momentous Labour. I remember your saying that you had notions of a good Genius presiding over you. I have of late had the same thought, for things which I do at Random are afterwards confirmed by my judgment in a dozen features of Propriety. Is it too daring to fancy Shakespeare this Presider? "[1]

The incidents that follow upon the appearance of Mercury and the mounting of Endymion and his companion on the jet-black steeds, though they may be considered conflicting and pointless so far as the mere story is concerned, are full of significance as a revelation of the working of the poet's mind. They include the flagging of the steeds at the approach of Sleep; the dream of Endymion, and his waking consciousness of the presence of his divine love; his perplexity as he turns now to her, now to the maiden beside him, and feels drawn alike to both, yet convinced that he is not unfaithful to either. Then comes the effort that Endymion makes to rouse the steeds again; the rising of the moon; the vanishing of the Indian maid, and the entry of Endymion into the Cave of Quietude.

In attempting to trace the significance of these incidents we may, for the sake of clearness, think of them

The incidents of the flight

as a personal reminiscence.

1 Letter of 10th May, 1817.

76

in the first place as representing a personal experience of the poet on some single occasion. Starting then a little further back than the series of events outlined above, we may picture him as sitting one evening, and allowing his thoughts to centre round " the agonies, the strife of human hearts," until he is led to wonder whether after all it were not better to try to do something to alleviate this suffering rather than to struggle on in the apparently hopeless effort to win fame as a poet. But before long his thoughts are touched as by an inspiration from heaven. " He always saw ideas embodied," as Mr. Bradley justly remarks.[1] His imagination is roused, and still keeping in mind the thought that had been with him before, he is carried aloft with a rush, and sees it all in a different light, under new aspects. Tired with the imaginative strain he feels sleep coming upon him, and, though he still tries to see more clearly what he is striving after, he does not succeed, and falling into unconsciousness he begins to dream. His dream follows the line, not of his meditations of the moment, but of the ideas that have for a long time dominated his outlook upon life ; he fancies that he has achieved his ideals as a poet, and that he has been found worthy to join the company of those whom he has reverenced as gods ; he can take part in their life and can a little use their instruments.[2] It is but a dream, and yet when he wakes it seems at first as if it were true, and he feels that this power is really his ; he is indeed a poet! What has become of his desire to serve mankind? Must this be abandoned? In perplexity he turns

[1] *Oxford Lectures on Poetry*, p. 217.
[2] There is a poem entitled *A Draught of Sunshine* (ed. Sélincourt, p. 353), which Keats sent to Reynolds in a letter of 31st January, 1818— the same letter in which he wrote out one of his most beautiful sonnets, " When I have fears that I may cease to be." *Endymion* was at this time passing through the press and was receiving some final touches. It is probable that these lines refer to this part of the story, and thus have more point and value than has yet been allowed to them.

from one ideal to the other, feeling that he is bound to follow each of them, yet not knowing how they can be reconciled. He calls to mind the flight of imagination which, before he fell asleep, had so magically uplifted these aspirations for service, and tries to renew this aspect of his thoughts, but a gleam of the old poetic desires that had so long haunted him comes into his mind; his passion to do something for humanity falls away, and, exhausted by the conflict of emotion through which he has passed he sinks into a dreamless sleep.

It is not, of course, intended to suggest that the experiences here outlined were necessarily confined to a single occasion; it may well have been that the desire to give some practical kind of help towards the relief of human suffering developed gradually in the mind of Keats; that there was more than one occasion on which the poetical impulse that was never far beneath the surface of his consciousness, acting on this desire, lifted it up into the region of creative imagination, and that periods of exhaustion and moods of apathy intervened. The significance of the story is not bound up with any particular time scheme. But whether it pictures for us the experience of a single occasion, or one that was spread over some longer period of time, it represents a phase in the process of Keats's poetic development, and one that he regards as of more than personal significance.

The wedding guests. While Endymion lay unconscious in the Cave of Quietude there passed by " A skyey mask, a pinion'd multitude " (558). They sang a song in celebration of the coming marriage feast of Diana.

We are probably intended to understand by this the attitude, not so much of the general public, as of that section of it which has a genuine interest in poetry, and which recognises the early dawn of a new era, such as the

78

New Romantic Movement in poetry. Among such as these there may be confidence and rejoicing at a time when the poet himself who has given cause for such feelings is still far from regarding his hopes as satisfied or his aims as accomplished. He may indeed be very little conscious of the interest and pleasure that others are taking in his work.

Soon after this Endymion's steed descended; he found himself once more on the solid earth, and close at hand was the Indian maid. The dreams that he had cherished, the ideals after which he had striven, now appeared to him unreal, or at least hopeless of attainment; and he declared that he would put them aside and devote himself whole-heartedly to the service of his new-found love. But to his unutterable dismay she told him that this could not be; no such end to his perplexity and trouble was possible. He knew not how to answer her, and while he sat in a stupor of grief and despair Peona came to greet them. _{Endymion returns to earth.}

There is little difficulty in the interpretation of this part of the story, if we follow the track that has led us thus far. After a prolonged and lofty flight of the imagination a reaction is bound to follow; the poet must inevitably come down to earth again and once more find himself in contact with the troubles and pains of human life. And if these have before aroused his solicitude and sympathy, in the mood of such a reaction their appeal will be stronger than ever. Poetry, especially on the side of beauty of form and expression, may seem for the time an unpractical pursuit, especially if, after trying for long months and years to attain to lofty ideals, the poet is conscious that he has always fallen short of them. _{The poet and practical life.}

> I have clung
> To nothing, lov'd a nothing, nothing seen
> Or felt but a great dream! (IV. 636)

So he turns with a sigh of relief to a more direct and more practical way of helping mankind. The desires and ambitions that he has so long cherished appear now to be hopelessly unattainable, and he resolves that he will no longer be guilty of the folly of pursuing them.

> Against his proper glory
> Has my own soul conspired: so my story
> Will I to children utter, and repent.
> There never liv'd a mortal man, who bent
> His appetite beyond his natural sphere,
> But starv'd and died.[1] My sweetest Indian, here,
> Here will I kneel, for thou redeemed hast
> My life from too thin breathing: gone and past
> Are cloudy phantasms. Caverns lone, farewell!
> And air of visions, and the monstrous swell
> Of visionary seas! No, never more
> Shall airy voices cheat me to the shore
> Of tangled wonder, breathless and aghast.
> Adieu, my daintiest Dream! although so vast
> My love is still for thee. The hour may come
> When we shall meet in pure elysium.
> On earth I may not love thee.   (IV. 643)

But however welcome such a cutting of the Gordian knot may seem for the moment as a relief from the doubts and perplexities that he has been trying to face, no such resolve can be a permanent solution of his difficulties. The call of the divine ideal has been too clear, the response has been too spontaneous, the efforts to reach the ideal have been too intense, to be abandoned in this way, and humanity itself cannot accept of service rendered at such a cost; it would involve an unfaithfulness that could but lead to death; and the poet is for a time thrown back upon his perplexities and uncertainties.

Returning to the scene of the early visions.

There is some significance in the fact that, at this point of the story, Endymion is back again, though he is unconscious of it, in the very spot where he had first seen the vision that had called him out from the ordinary life

[1] In a similar mood he wrote to Haydon (11th May, 1817): " There is no greater Sin after the seven deadly than to flatter oneself into an idea of being a great Poet."

of men.   The long process of training through which
Endymion had passed could not of itself make him a
poet.   Before that end could be attained he must return
to the source of inspiration that had given the original
impulse to his new way of life.   This is the essential
element in the whole process, without which all the rest,
useful and even necessary as it may be, must fail of its
effect, for it is this inspiration that alone gives life and
power to the words of the poet.

The last occasion on which we heard of Peona was Peona.
when she tried to soothe the spirit of Endymion, troubled
by the early visions that he had seen, and to draw him
back to his former natural and healthy manner of life
(I. 991).   During the period of his strange, fantastic
wanderings he has been far out of her ken, but now that
he has returned once more to the scenes of his earlier
youth she comes to him with glad welcome, and rejoices
in the hope of his resuming a more normal mode of life.
There is nothing selfish in her attitude; she welcomes with
open heart the beautiful stranger, but completely misin-
terprets the situation, and is reduced to bewildered
amazement when Endymion puts all her hopeful sugges-
tions on one side, declaring that he will live a hermit life,
and that Peona herself shall be his only visitant.

The strange *impasse* to which the adventures of The perplexity
of rival claims
Endymion have led appears to represent in a large
measure the personal experience of Keats, though the
general situation has a wider meaning.   There seems to
have been a time when he was greatly perplexed and
harassed in his outlook upon life.   On the one hand
the desire of making his name live in the ranks of the
poets was very strong within him; on the other he was
oppressed by the pains and sorrows of his fellow men, and
longed to devote himself to their service.   In the days

when he was working as a medical student " Poetry was to his mind the zenith of all his aspirations the only thing worthy the attention of superior minds "—such is the record of one of his fellow students, already quoted.[1] But a little later we find him writing : " I find there is no worthy pursuit but the idea of doing some good to the world."[2]   And it would appear that for a time he could see no way of reconciling the two ideals. He was drawn most powerfully towards each of them, so much so that he could not without pain think of forsaking either; yet for the time it seemed that he could not follow them both; he must choose between them.   Still less was it possible to return to the ordinary life of men from which he had felt himself to be separated ever since he had seen the vision of poetic beauty.   And so a feeling of depression settled down upon him; his ideals were unattainable; a return to his former life was impossible.   There seemed to be no way out of the tangle of contradiction. He was inclined to seek for peace in solitude, and to abandon both ideals as being beyond his reach.   Yet he could find no satisfaction in such a decision.   To cut himself off from the aims and aspirations that had lifted him above the ordinary ways of men would not give rest to his soul. Thus far it may be that we have been shown how the struggle and perplexity worked in the mind of Keats.

The denouement is finely conceived, and pictures for us a truth of universal significance

Endymion, feeling the impossibility of cutting himself off thus from all that he had longed for, begged Peona to bring the Indian maid that evening to meet him once more; they were to come to the groves behind the temple of Diana.   So strongly did he feel the futility of all his

[1] See p. 23, Colvin, *Life of Keats*, p. 31.
[2] To John Taylor, 24th April, 1818.   This letter reads as if he had recently cleared up the difficulty referred to above.

hopes and efforts that at one moment he was ready to welcome death, though at another it seemed a cruel end to what he knew had been at least a sincere striving towards the light. In this mood he approached the temple, and met Peona and the Indian maid. When Peona asked him what was to happen next, his answer showed that he had reached some solution of his doubts and perplexities —the solution, that is, of willingness to submit entirely to the guidance of a higher power : The resolving of the perplexity.

> " Sister, I would have command,
> If it were heaven's will, on our sad fate." (IV. 975)

And then the final revelation is granted to him, and he learns to his amazement and joy that the goddess whom he has so long pursued, but has never fully known, and the Indian maiden who has called out his passionate devotion, are not rivals for his love, but are different aspects of the same being, whom he now knows in truth, and to whom he will henceforth be joined in deathless delight.

So it is, Keats would tell us, when the poet comes to realise that his longing aspirations after beauty and perfection in his poetry, and his passionate desire to serve his fellow creatures, are not conflicting ideals, but are one and the same; that for him to use faithfully and earnestly his poetic gift is to render the highest service to mankind; then he has become a true poet.

It is a pleasant little touch that Peona is not shut out from a share in this joyful climax, though she fails to comprehend its meaning. The poet's ways are in a large measure ways where others cannot follow him, yet he does not lose touch with their life; and the men and women—not a small company—to whom poetry is little better than sounding brass or a tinkling cymbal, and who find it incomprehensible that a lifetime should be devoted Peona's share.

to it, may yet have some share in the beauty and joy that it brings into human life.

The introduction to the fourth book.

The introduction to this book dwells on the way in which English poetry, refusing to be merely imitative of even the best of what other lands could offer, waited until the time had come to develop its own genius; and Keats feels that the new movement in poetry, with the celebration of which this poem is largely concerned, represents the full fruition of the hopes that had so long been waiting for fulfilment. The note thus sounded is in harmony with the triumphant close to which the story finally attains.

CPSIA information can be obtained
at www.ICGtesting.com
Printed in the USA
LVHW090412121019
634026LV00001B/114/P